MILES

*A Portrait of the 17th
Duke of Norfolk*

MILES

A Portrait of the 17th Duke of Norfolk

GERARD NOEL

MICHAEL RUSSELL

© Gerard Noel and contributors as cited 2004

First published in Great Britain 2004
by Michael Russell (Publishing) Ltd
Wilby Hall, Wilby, Norwich NR16 2JP

Typeset in Sabon by Waveney Typesetters
Wymondham, Norfolk
Printed and bound in Great Britain
by Biddles Ltd, King's Lynn, Norfolk

ISBN 0 85955 289 6

Contents

Foreword

I am very glad that Gerard Noel has written this book about Miles Norfolk. To those of us who knew him well, he was a remarkable man. Soldier, landowner, banker, Earl Marshal and, above all, a family man. Happily married to Anne for fifty-three years.

That of course tells you very little about Miles as a person. It is difficult to capture the essence of someone's personality on paper, but in this book some of the notes which Miles wrote and the anecdotes told about him show something of his qualities.

I first met Miles before the war, when we were brother officers. Second Lieutenant Miles Fitzalan Howard was indistinguishable from Miles, 17th Duke of Norfolk. Unpretentious, amusing, modest, much-liked and respected, an excellent soldier, who subsequently had a distinguished career in the Army. A man of firm opinions and unafraid to air them. Respectful of authority, up to a point, but quite ready to challenge and confront it when he thought it unreasonable or wrong. There was, as is recounted in this book, an occasion when he described an edict from on high as 'damned nonsense'. There was a good deal of consternation of this language coming from so important a person. He subsequently issued a statement saying that 'damned nonsense was a military way of saying that he didn't entirely agree'. He never trimmed his sails or adjusted his manner to whomever he was speaking, whether it was a fellow duke or a dustman. All were alike and equal, deserving of the same courtesy, attention and regard.

Miles was, very properly, immensely proud of his family and their long tradition of service to this country. He felt he had a privileged position and, because of that, an obligation to public service for his country, for his regiment and for those who worked for him, or for whom he was responsible. All his life he discharged those responsibilities.

To those of us who knew him well and held him in much affection, this book will be lasting reminder of his unique personality.

CARRINGTON

Acknowledgements

When expressing my thanks for the help I have received in producing this portrait of Miles Norfolk, I will begin, if I may, with the very embryo of the book. I can thus include certain people who, even at that early stage, were extremely helpful to me in various ways; and I apologise if this involves a recital of thanks which is inevitably somewhat personal.

We were spending a very happy holiday with Miles and Anne at Rawlins Plantation in the West Indian island of St Kitts when, more or less by accident, the book took on its earliest form.

I had known and admired Miles ever since I was about seven and he was about eighteen, and it was a sudden inspiration during that holiday in St Kitts which made me realise what an attractive subject for a biography his life would be. On the other hand I might seem presumptuous in proposing myself as its author.

I discussed the embryonic idea with my wife Adele. She was nearly as old a friend of Anne as I was of Miles, and she wisely stressed the need for discretion and sensitivity. That advice and all her help and encouragement at later stages have been factors for which I am infinitely grateful. Indeed, without Adele the book would never even have been begun, let alone completed.

Then one afternoon – virtually, as I say, by accident – something happened that had the eventual effect of setting the book in motion. I was sitting with Miles after lunch when I casually asked 'I suppose, Miles, you were born at Carlton?'

'Oh no,' he replied, 'I was born at 49 Eaton Place.'

And then, with little or no prompting from myself, he continued by saying 'It was my Aunt Vi's house. She was my great-uncle's wife. My parents were actually living in Manchester Square at the time.'

And so the narrative went on, crammed with interest about Miles's family and early life and accompanied by a recital of details that revealed his extraordinary memory. His narrative was uninterruptedly fluent and the events were recalled as of yesterday.

This is how it all began. There was no question of telling Miles that I had any intention, however vague at that point, of writing his life. There was equally no conspiratorial plan to mislead him in any way. Indeed, I had not formulated any plan about a book. Everything was being played by ear.

It so happened that our small party at Rawlins Plantation that winter included Carol Costello, a most charming American cousin of Anne's; Elizabeth Bonn, a cousin of mine (her maiden name being Buxton) and also of Anne's; and a very old friend of mine as well as of the Norfolks, Bill Birch Reynardson. All of them, in slightly different ways, were most helpful. Carol, having known Anne for so long, felt a book would be an admirable idea and something that, one day, Anne would like. For the time being however it was advisable, she thought, to take a very long term view. I quite agreed.

Elizabeth also, quite rightly, advised caution but urged me to make as many notes as I could of my conversations with Miles.

Bill gave some very shrewd advice along similar lines and, even while we were still in St Kitts, read through some pages I produced based on what Miles had told me and made useful suggestions. I had known Bill since we were called to the Bar together, and he has known Anne for ages and lives near her in Oxfordshire. He has been of great assistance to me in many important ways.

It goes without saying that my principal indebtedness is to Anne herself. When, in November 2003, I ventured to approach Anne on the subject, she most generously agreed to the project and has been continuously and substantially helpful to me ever since. As the sub-title makes clear, this book is a 'Portrait' rather than a conventional or complete, let alone strictly chronological, biography.

I am scarcely less grateful to other members of Miles's family, especially his youngest brother Mark, who has always given me special encouragement and support.

Cardinal Cormac Murphy O'Connor, Archbishop of Westminster, most magnanimously allowed his Throne Room at Archbishop's House to be used as the venue for a reception to mark the publication of the book.

I had not got far with the actual writing before realising that although I had long known Miles well as a friend, my personal knowledge of his career as a soldier, which formed so central a part of his life, was woefully inadequate. It was thus that Tony Chambers, who is married to Anne's sister Rosemary and is himself a one-time Grenadier, took on the task of researching and writing this very important aspect of the story.

John Martin Robinson, Miles's close friend and scholarly archivist at Arundel Castle, has also played a vital role in the completion of the book. He carefully looked through an early text and made many editorial suggestions. His corrections and additions regarding Norfolk family history were invaluable and he is the author of the Epilogue about Miles's official life.

The late Philip Daniel, a close collaborator of Miles at the Catholic Union of Great Britain, an old friend of mine, gave me a lot of help and information as to this aspect of Miles's work.

With regard to Miles's participation in the proceedings of the House of Lords, I must acknowledge the contribution of several people, notably Alan Bell, formerly the Librarian of the London Library. With the help of members of his staff, and also of the assistant librarian of the House of Lords, he made it possible for me to have access to dates, statistics and vital information relating to Miles's interventions in the House of Lords debates, based on Hansard, as well to as some of his other activities in the Upper House.

I owe a very special and personal debt of gratitude to my sister Maureen who has known Miles ever since they, along with Michael and Mariegold, grew up together in the late 1920s and 1930s. Maureen has excellent recall and recounted numerous adventures that took place at Carlton before the war, as well as giving me the benefit of wider recollections. I particularly enjoyed our conversations, just as talking about her old friends, she told me, brought back happy memories for her.

I am very grateful to Father Benet Perceval, OSB, a close friend of Miles at Ampleforth and still a member of the community there. He most kindly welcomed me when I visited him at Ampleforth, and gave me some valuable notes as well as lending me some interesting photographs of Miles in his young days.

I am deeply appreciative that Lord Carrington has done me the kindness of supplying a Foreword to the book. His long friendship with

Miles, combined with the pre-eminent distinction of his own life and career, give his contribution particular resonance.

I am conscious of the fact that there are others in whose debt I stand but whom I have not mentioned by name, other than in the course of the text. I apologise for this omission which in no way lessens my gratitude. I have been vitally encouraged and helped from these quarters and extend my thanks to all concerned. We all evidently share a lasting affection and admiration for Miles.

PART ONE

Student

I
Upbringing

Miles Francis Stapleton Fitzalan Howard was born on 21 July 1915 at 49 Eaton Place, London, in the house of his 'Aunt Vi' as he always called her. This Lady Beaumont was the widow of Henry, 9th Lord Beaumont, and was actually Miles's great-aunt. Miles always spoke with affection of Aunt Vi, but the same could not be said of his memories of her late husband. Miles was never unreasonably critical of people and generally had nothing but praise for his ancestors. He made an exception, however, in the case of that particular great-uncle (Henry Stapleton, 9th Lord Beaumont). He had, according to Miles, married Aunt Vi for her money, having spent all his own money on Carlton Towers. She was the only daughter of Frederick Wootton Isaacson, MP, and the famous Mayfair milliner Madame Elise.

Miles's parents, Lord Howard of Glossop (always known as 'Bar') and Baroness Beaumont, had married in August 1914 at the Beaumont family home, Carlton Towers, in what was then the East Riding of Yorkshire (now North Yorkshire). They had a large, rambling London house in Manchester Square, near the Wallace Collection, and round the corner from the Catholic church of St James's, Spanish Place, which – as devout Catholics – they regularly attended. Although they were very happy in the Manchester Square house (now pulled down), they felt it would not be conveniently situated for the birth of their first child; so Miles's mother, Mona, moved to the Beaumont house in Eaton Place for the period of her confinement.

Her son was christened at St Mary's Church, Cadogan Street, and given the names Miles and Francis after his two grandfathers. That he was to be addressed as Miles rather upset his (Francis) Howard grandfather, who always referred to Miles as Mills, presumably to annoy Mona. (The further name Stapleton was added at the special request of Mona.) Soon after the christening the family moved back to Manchester Square.

Miles's earliest memories were of being almost constantly with his

brother Michael, fifteen months younger than himself, and his younger
sister Mariegold, at Carlton or at 15 Manchester Square. They went to
Farm Street Church to be instructed in the Catholic faith and made
their first Communion in the Lady Chapel there with Father Woodlock,
a famous Jesuit whom I remember well from my own youth. They
normally went to Sunday Mass to St James's, Spanish Place, where
Bishop Butt lived and it was he who adamantly advised that the boys
should be sent to Ampleforth rather than Eton, despite Miles's Tempest
grandmother's opinion that Eton could not be bettered.

Miles's mother had a passion for the boys to be in the open air at all
times and they went to the Open Air School in the Botanical Gardens,
Regent's Park. They were only allowed to go on the top of the open
buses and never into a cinema or any other enclosed building. Shoes,
bought from Daniel Neal in Portman Square, had to be fitted on the
pavement because Nanny Johnston (of whom more later) had been
made to promise never to take the boys inside a shop.

Later, Miles and Michael went to Gaveney House Day School in the
Finchley Road. Nanny Johnston arrived in May 1925, a formidable but
kindly figure whom I remember well from the many mutual tea-parties.
She was later joined by an assistant nanny, Annie Ferguson, and later
still by a nurserymaid called Jessie. Lady Beaumont employed an additional nurserymaid who was French. This was so that the boys could
learn French 'unconsciously'. Michael and Miles, however, as the latter
ruefully confesses in his written memories of those early years, were
'utterly vile to her and I can remember, even now, sticking safety-pins
into her so as to make her unhappy and leave'. ('Now I regret', he adds,
'that I had not learned fluent French painlessly and always feel guilty at
our behaviour.')

Around the corner from where Miles was born in Eaton Square,
there lived Miles's cousin, Edmund, Viscount Fitzalan of Derwent, the
last ever Viceroy of Ireland. He was soon to become England's leading
lay spokesman on Catholic affairs. This came about because the Duke
of Norfolk of the day, Bernard Marmaduke, Miles's cousin, was still a
minor, having succeeded to the title at the age of nine in 1917. Bernard,
in due course, became a respected Earl Marshal but was never so
closely interested in Catholic affairs as Miles. Educated at the Oratory,
he had a lifelong interest in cricket and racing on the one hand, and
court ceremony on the other; but Miles paid high tribute also to

Bernard's scrupulous concern for Catholic affairs. The cricket matches at Arundel were a well-known feature and Bernard also took a postwar MCC team to Australia. Many years later, in the early Seventies, he was the sponsor to the internationally famous cricket star Learie Constantine, originally from Trinidad, when the latter took his seat in the House of Lords as the first peer of black African descent. In matters of court ceremony Bernard became an expert. He was also chief steward of the Jockey Club and the Queen's Representative at Royal Ascot.

He had four daughters but no son, and the heir to the dukedom for many years was the Lord Fitzalan just mentioned. His son, Henry, was the next heir to the dukedom but he also had daughters and no son. It was thus that Miles, though only a relatively distant cousin, became heir apparent to the dukedom to which he succeeded in 1975. The year 2000 marked his eighty-fifth birthday, and his twenty-fifth year as Duke of Norfolk. Ironically, his wife Anne, born Constable Maxwell, whom he married in 1949, was closer to the main Norfolk line than was Miles himself. Bernard's mother having been a Constable Maxwell.

Miles's 'Aunt Vi' has already been mentioned in connection with the house in Eaton Place where Miles was born. Her husband, Henry Stapleton, 9th Lord Beaumont, died without issue on 23 January 1892, and his brother Miles became the 10th Lord Beaumont. He, in 1869, had reverted from Anglicanism to the Roman Catholicism of his family, thus reversing the action of his father, yet another Miles, the 8th Lord Beaumont, taken in 1850 in protest at the manner of the restoration of the Catholic hierarchy in England and Wales.

Miles lived at Carlton for most of his early life. It was and is, though magnificent and originally of medieval foundation, a monument to the Victorian Gothic period of architecture at its highest point. People said it looked like St Pancras Station without the trains. Some considered this a description of Carlton's ugliness while, to others, no description could have been more flattering. It had first been built as Carlton Hall and then renovated by Miles's great-uncle Henry. Enormous though it is, the original design dictated that it should have been even larger, but despite the marriage to the Isaacson heiress, the money eventually ran out.

Miles Stapleton, 10th Lord Beaumont, brother of Henry, 9th Lord Beaumont, married comparatively late after an adventurous career as a soldier. Between 1874 and 1895 he served with the 20th Hussars in

Canada, Malta, Bechuanaland and, gaining important military honours, with the Egyptian Frontier Field Force. In 1893, at the age of forty-three, he married Ethel Mary, daughter of Sir Charles Henry Tempest. Because of her fortune Carlton Towers and the family remained solvent.

In the August of the following year, his first child, Mona, was born and before the end of 1895 his wife was again pregnant. Never having made a will, he decided that now was the time to do so. His testamentary wishes were ready for signature on 16 September 1895, a month before his second child was due. Lord Beaumont was ever anxious, at this time of the year, to get out with his gun to look for rabbits in the grounds of Carlton, the shooting season proper not yet having started. The will was executed as early in the day as was convenient for the two required witnesses, shortly after which he was off on his morning ramble. While climbing a stile, he was accidentally killed by his own gun, thus surviving by only a couple of hours the execution of his last will and testament. It took the family a long time to get over the shock.

Though the title could be inherited through the female line in the absence of a male heir, the infant, Mona, was still only heir presumptive, final inheritance depending on the sex of the next child to be born. The barony thus went temporarily into abeyance. A month later (4 October 1895) a girl, Ivy (later Mrs Jerry Micklethwait), was born. Somewhat protracted formalities followed before the abeyance could be lifted and it was not until 1 June 1896 that Mona became Baroness Beaumont in her own right. She was thus, as Miles put it many years later, 'squireen' of Carlton for almost the whole of her long life, her death occurring in 1971. Carlton was always her dream home, and so became, to some extent, Miles's as well.

Unfortunately, however, or – as some would say – fortunately, the money ran out during the original construction of the house and further building had to be discontinued. It is thus – and this became something of a Fitzalan Howard family joke – that a large, high-ceilinged gallery forms the beginning of what might have been an extensive east wing. At the end of the gallery are some massive double doors which look as if they will open up to another large room. Instead of this, when opened, they reveal only a brick wall. It was at this point that the house came to an abrupt end, and all further building was discontinued.

Miles spent his very happy formative years here and was never over-awed by the atmosphere and physical appearance which some people find somewhat heavy and oppressive about Carlton. In later years it combined a strictly old-fashioned interior and regime, with the usual scarcity of bathrooms and absence of heating, with one or two surprisingly modern innovations. It was one of the first houses of its kind, for example, to be equipped with a telephone, the number being Snaith 43.

When they got married, Bar and Mona came to an agreement to live at Carlton and be buried at Glossop, but Bar sold Glossop after the First World War. It was turned into a school and later demolished. Miles's roots were thus firmly sunk in the West Riding of Yorkshire. The Stapletons and their ancestors had lived at Carlton since Norman times. In recent years it has been lived in and looked after by Miles's younger son, Gerald, who, with his wife Emma, has done a splendid job in keeping up Carlton in a way that would have made Miles proud.

To the end of his life Miles confirmed his time there had been 'idyllic' and the whole of the next chapter is devoted to a description of the Carlton years in Miles's own words.

Carlton: 'At the Back of the Vinery'

This chapter exactly reproduces in Miles's own words his early memories of days at his beloved Carlton, and other scenes of his youth. He collected them together in November 1982 under the title 'At the Back of the Vinery'.

Whenever broken ornaments or furniture had to be discarded, it was always to the back of the Vinery greenhouse and this is where my brother Michael and I, and subsequent brothers and sisters, had such fun, because we could be untidy, away from the prying eyes of our nannies, mother and grandmother. Michael and I, for instance, once had a marvellous bonfire which went through drainage pipes, which we discovered lying around, and came out smoking 20 yards in the woods. Another time we dug for coal – and found it after 4 or 5 feet – for there had been an old coal dump!

We could get dirty but always had to be washed for our meals, especially when we grew older and came down to the dining-room. If a visitor came, there were napkins, but we were never allowed to use them, having to put them beside our plates and save the laundry bill. When Michael and I woke up in the morning we used to take it in turns to dirty the water with a bit of soap in the basin so that Annie and Nanny would think we had washed.

My sisters Miriam and Miranda have told me they were not allowed to walk on the front stairs' carpet but had to walk on the wood at the side so as to save wearing out the carpet, but I can never remember this. Another fetish of my mother and grandmother was to re-use envelopes and write letters on any blank area of paper, even if the other side was already used, so that when the stringent wartime economies on the re-use of envelopes and paper occurred, they were well prepared for it.

On rainy days we would stay in the day nursery and often play trains, running round the nursery table. Michael and I both pretended to be the Flying Scotsman, and Mariegold would try to join in and got in our way, so we used to pretend she was a goods train and shunt her into the corner as a siding; but she soon came out again. Later, Mariegold had a child's methylated spirits cooker and, one day, while we were filling it up, the can caught on fire, which was then dropped by Michael or me and the whole nursery floor was in a sheet of flame. One of us ran into one of the night nurseries and got the jug of cold water off the washstand and poured it on top of this fire, which merely had the effect of setting the wainscot alight around the whole room. Fortunately, Annie came in and scolded us severely and ably put out the fire by using the fireside rug to suffocate it, but we nearly burnt Carlton down and were more careful in future.

Martin used to hold his breath to gain more attention when he cried and we were told he might suffocate and kill himself. But he played the trick so often that we got tired and evolved another system of stopping him, by pouring one of the jugs of cold water over him which quickly brought him to breathe again.

Nanny Johnston was a most determined and imposing character and it was she who determined where we would go for our annual fortnight at the sea. She decided whether we would go to Westgate or Felixstowe and would then tell Mummy and also the Norfolk nanny of the decision and the Drummond Nanny so that Cousin Gwen Norfolk and Cousin Ela Perth would know where to book rooms for Katharine and Winnie Howard, and Margaret and Gillian Drummond respectively.

Whenever there was a thunderstorm we had the knives quickly collected from the nursery table and taken to the pantry, because they were of steel and Nanny thought that steel would attract lightning and we might all get killed. Similarly, I can remember being told not to stand under any lone oak tree in the Park, because they also attracted lightning, which indeed was true and more sensible but one got very wet as a result.

When I was very young, I can remember two or three laundry-maids washing the sheets and household linen, squeezing out the water with wonderful wooden mangles. The laundry was in what became, for many years, the gun room next door to the stoke hole, where there was a great copper heated by a special fire. The sheets were finally carried in baskets to the drying green, where we later built an aviary. But eventually the laundry was closed down and the dirty linen used to be sent to a convent in Leeds in large wicker hampers.

Granny had necessarily to be economical for she had bought back Carlton with Tempest money, which she had inherited as the only daughter of Sir Charles Tempest, her father, because the 9th Lord Beaumont had died bankrupt with the rebuilding. His wife, Aunt Violet, had moved to Slindon in Sussex with one third of the Carlton furniture and some pictures, which were always meant to be left back to the family, but not all of it succeeded in surviving the war; however, most of the pictures returned. We had to go down to the post office to telephone, until my grandmother was very ill in 1931 and the telephone was installed in the room off the dining-room. There were only two bathrooms, the nursery bathroom and the green one at the end of the state passage. This had been put in when my grandmother came to the house on her marriage in 1894 and before that there were only hip baths. Old houses used to have buckets as earth closets in odd, out-of-the-way rooms where the smell would not be so obnoxious. And so, when water closets were invented, these were made into water closet lavatories, which meant that water had to be laid on to the most remote places without any reference to sensible plumbing as we now know it. For instance, there was the nursery lavatory in the little room over the stone stairs, there was the lavatory at the top of the front stairs, called Aunt Ivy's lavatory, and there was an even more remote one at the top of the little circular staircase which contained a bell. This bell was rung regularly at 12.30 to summon the servants for their midday meal, but if tolled at another time it signified an emergency and the gardeners were then meant to go to the house in case there was a fire.

Electric light had been put in the house in 1914 and was made by a marvellous anthracite gas engine which charged up batteries, which provided 100-volts electric light. These frequently went dim and could only provide current for a small number of lights, so there was a genuine need to economise by 'clicking off the light' after it had been used. Curiously the light switches were hidden at the backs of doors in remote places. In the morning room, the lamps were brought in when darkness fell at 4 o'clock and the plants or vases of flowers were taken out. It was thought shabby to leave lamps in the room in the morning and afternoon, which must have been a relic of the essential habit of oil lamps having to be trimmed and refilled each morning.

My grandmother felt she was most economical in only having Adler, the butler, and a footman who used to carry up the dining-room meals on a tray, and a hall boy who used to carry up our nursery meals on a tray. Adler always changed into a white tie for dinner and, when Michael and I grew older, we came down to dinner always in a black tie and a stiff shirt. There were only two house parties a year; one for York races and, two weeks later, for Doncaster races (St Leger) when an additional butler called Mr Slack was hired from Doncaster. Then there was champagne and wine and port served, otherwise very little was drunk, since my mother and grandmother never drank at all, but my father had a glass of whisky each night. Much of the house was permanently closed and any room not used was always covered in dust sheets.

We occasionally had a children's party with a great fire in the Venetian drawing-room and a Christmas tree with real candles which Adler extinguished with a wet sponge on the end of a stick before the whole tree caught fire, which it nearly did so often. Otherwise, the Venetian drawing-room and picture gallery were in perpetual dust sheets except for the annual servants' ball and the Badsworth Hunt Ball. Joe Hinsley, the second senior gardener, a cousin of Cardinal Hinsley, told me that in his early days the servants' ball took place in the servants' hall on stone flags and he used to nearly wear out a pair of shoes dancing, and how kind it was of Her Ladyship to allow them to dance in the Venetian drawing-room in later years.

The opening meet of the Badsworth Hunt was always held at Carlton, and when we were young Michael and I used to ride, our first pony being called Pig-in-the-Poke. But as soon as we became old enough to shoot, we gave up riding to the great sadness of my grandmother. Granny and my Aunt Ivy both rode side-saddle and were very determined and courageous. They would always go to the most expensive tailors for their riding habit. Otherwise they economised on all their dresses. There was a lady's maid who looked after my grandmother and Aunt Ivy; and Mummy, after she was married, had a lady's maid of her own. Their dresses were all kept in the large green wardrobe in what is now called the cupboard bedroom.

There were three housemaids, a cook, a kitchen maid and a scullery maid. The old kitchen floor was Yorkshire flags like the present back passage and it was scrubbed or mopped each day by the scullery maid. I can remember Granny's pride at having found the money to have it tiled, as it now is, and also the still-room across the passage where the cakes were made, so as to ease the burden of this terrible daily chore.

The gardener, called Spencer, used to wheel the coke to the central heating boiler under the harp room and also to the hot water boilers, which still exist but are disused, near the back door. He would also carry the coal upstairs to the great iron rectangular tubs from which the housemaids used to refill the coal scuttles for the bedrooms. He was also responsible for mopping the back passage once a week. Adler, the butler, and the head housemaid and cook had their meals in the housekeeper's room, now the television room, and the others in the servants' hall; except that for the sweet course Granny's lady's maid, called Teal, and Mummy's, called Franckton, curiously came along the back passage with their glass and spoon and fork to have the sweet course in the housekeeper's room.

There was much silver out in the morning room and some in the dining-room, which was cleaned by Adler every day in the pantry and I can hear now the noise of his cufflinks rattling against his starched cuffs as he rolled up his sleeves to do the polishing.

The dinners at the York and Doncaster race parties were really very grand with all the silver out on the dining-room table, wonderful peaches and white grapes which had been specially produced from the greenhouses, and one night the silver-gilt would all be out with yellow flowers to match. After we had played vingt-et-un or some other game we would go to bed and Adler would be in the armoury at the bottom of the stairs ready to give each guest a silver candlestick, already alight, so that he or she could find their way to the bedroom. This was before electric torches were produced and there was no question of having electric lights always on in the passages. The system would simply not have stood such a consumption of electricity. For the races the bow drawing-room was taken out of its dust sheets and even the Sheffield plate hinges on the silver front door were taken off, one at a time, and polished by Adler so that, towards the end, only brass remained.

Each morning the *Yorkshire Post* and *Morning Post* arrived but *The Times* came to Snaith station by 11 o'clock and had to be fetched by John Davies, the groom, on a bicycle. Later we also had the *Daily Mirror* so as to be able to follow 'Pip, Squeak and Wilfred'.

Mr Nichols was head gardener, living in the present keeper's cottage across the Park, near the Mill Lane. Joe Hinsley, the second head, lived in a house just north of the Wesleyan Chapel, opposite the then post office. But the two we knew best were Spencer and Giles, who were older and always seemed to work together. They would tell how the rose garden was dug out in the 1870–80s and the soil spread out to make the large flat grass lawn bank to the west. They used to mow the lawn with an old grey mare who wore wonderful leather boots. Later a 'Greens' motor mower took over, operated by Willie Graves, a much younger gardener, who was married to the daughter of the head gardener, Mr Nichols. Peaches, grapes, nectarines, strawberries, melons and cucumbers were grown in the greenhouses and flowers forced ahead.

There was also Joe Shaw, a gypsy I believe, who is still alive, who used to syringe out the greenhouses every Saturday morning. We used to call him 'Little Joe' to distinguish him from Joe Hinsley, whom we called 'Big Joe'. Big Joe used to take the dog cart to Goole once a week to sell surplus fruit and vegetables in the market there. Little Joe used to wheel a barrow of vegetables to Snaith for the market there once a week and, since it was about a two-mile journey, he had a rod over his shoulders, attached to the handles, to lessen the weight on his arms. We were entirely self-supporting in fruit and vegetables, and ice cream was made for the race parties by importing a block of ice from Snaith. The arrival of the fridge and tinned food changed so much of this life. Before I was born, ice was taken from the floods along the Templehurst Road and stored in a circular brick pit in sawdust near the green door, which was the equivalent of an ice house.

During the year the two park men, George Leaf and 'Dummy' Leaf, would bring logs to the stable yard and pile them up against the house, against Adler's bedroom, which was the first room on the right by the back door next to the stoke hole and laundry. Once a year, the steam traction engine, which was also used by the farmers to do the threshing in their haystack yards, would come up and the circular saw would be borrowed from Bob Hinsley, the carpenter, and all those logs were sawn up for us in the house. It was a thrilling sight especially when the large logs were sawn up as gate posts and fencing. But about 1935 Granny spent £300 or £400 on having the whole of the Park boundary refenced with creosoted general fencing, which is still standing.

The gardens were kept meticulously and the gravel round the front of the house was raked every Saturday morning by hand, often before we were out of bed, for I think the gardeners started work at 7 each morning and worked till 5, with an hour break for lunch. The walks and gravel were weeded by hand, there being no weedkillers at the time and every year all the leaves were raked up and burnt in 'the walks', which the gardeners called the 'pleasure grounds'. I refer to the woods between the iron park fence and the long village wall.

We had two grass tennis courts on the lawn and, in the '30s, the hard tennis court was put down in the orchard, with a little summer house, built specially for Michael and me, added to the crazy paving in front of it. I can well remember the white tennis balls becoming green on the grass courts and Mummy and Aunt Ivy would scrub them clean on the door mats in the garden entrance next day after a tennis party had been held.

There was a small pond, about 20 yards across, in the Park, some 400 yards directly opposite the iron gate on the back drive. This pond no longer exists and has been ploughed over. We were told that it had no bottom and in years gone by a coach and horses had driven into it in the dark and had disappeared. You can imagine our surprise one day when we saw a cartwheel floating in the pond. So the story of the coach was true after all! Alas, we later discovered that the carpenter had made a new wheel for Joe Hinsley's dog-cart and was soaking it in the pond in order to make the wooden wheel expand to fit the metal tyre.

The Park was all grass-grazing and farmers paid so much a head for cattle and horses for the whole year; some small farmers had milking cows which were fetched by their children daily. 'Dummy' Leaf, who could not talk or hear, had a brother who looked after the Park fences and also ran the 'pump-house' near the lake and two boat houses, where the coal steam engine pumped the house water to the tank in the Flag Staff (Stapleton) Tower. Steam was in fact the only source of power for any factory like the clog mills in Snaith and the other factories in Selby. If the wind blew strong from the West Riding factories the sky could become black and some of the tree trunks were really black and smutty at Ardsley (near Barnsley) where Jerry Micklethwait lived. When Jerry married Aunty Ivy he started to live at Carlton with the card room as his study, but this proved a failure and so they moved to Ardsley House.

Michael and I learned to shoot with a .410, and then we each were given a 28 bore and later, on my 21st birthday, Daddy gave me my present pair of Purdey guns for which he paid £100 and I later discovered they had been made in 1898. Michael also had a pair given him.

We used to shoot rabbits endlessly and, one summer holiday, we snared 99 and never got the 100 even though we left our snares out and only took them up on the morning when we had to go back to Ampleforth. We also shot wood pigeons and once, when it was my turn, we saw a pheasant in L. Pond Wood on the ground. It had strayed in and this could not be missed so I shot my first pheasant on the ground! We also walked for miles after partridges and used to be dropped at Catbabbleton on the Selby road and walk back gradually by Port Jackson Farm, Rose Hill Farm and the allotments on the Templeton Road, returning to Carlton by lunch time. In the afternoon we would often then go and shoot the flying ground and the warpings down Mill Lane, near the river. These were so called because in the 18th century they would warp an area, which meant letting the river flow into it for two or three tides to deposit silt over the fields. Papa would always stride ahead and shout at us to keep up into line. They were great days with many more partridges, as there was no crop spraying and many more hedges. Mr Nichols used to come out shooting with a hammer gun and Mr Telfer followed George Leaf as the keeper/park man. We had to mark every bird and rush forward when it fell since we never had a dog. I think the record bag for one day was 36 brace of partridges.

We travelled to London in the brougham, always smelling of moth balls, to Snaith Station; by train to Knottingley, where we changed, than a second change at Doncaster and so to King's Cross where Daddy had ordered a station bus to meet us and drive us to Manchester Square. One year, when Mama and Papa were already in London, Michael and I were taken there from school by Mr Nichols, the head gardener. We travelled in the brougham to Templehurst Station and Mr Nichols had a box of peaches wrapped in cotton wool of which he took far more care than of us. They were destined for Granny's dinner party in London,

But we always returned from King's Cross to Selby, where we were again met by the brougham and the heavy trunks came on later on a dray specially hired by Granny. John Davies and his son Dennis looked after the four or five hunters in the loose boxes, which were where the present tractor workshop now operates. In the middle was the carriage house where the brougham and dog cart were kept and on the other side, on the site of what became a restaurant for many years, were stalls for the horses, for the brougham, the grey mare and later Fanny.

Granny also had a car (a Renault – later a series of Vauxhalls) which John drove most alarmingly. He always wore gaiters like any other chauffeur and had a yellow collar – an idea of Granny's so that she could spot him in a car park. When Michael and I first went to Ampleforth in May 1924, the Vauxhall failed to climb Brandsby Bank and we had to help it by getting out and walking up. My grandmother told me that, as a railway shareholder, she had the right to stop the train and used to get off at Templehurst, but that once it failed to do so and she was carried on to Selby, where she had to hire a cab. She sent the bill for this to the railway company!

In London we lived at 15 Manchester Square, which was too large for us and Daddy always felt the cracks in the nursery ceiling were serious and so he used to measure them by sticking pieces of stamp paper across them. The house did indeed collapse when bombed early in the Second World War. For the London Season, Granny and I used to come with some of the Carlton servants. Daddy had a dark blue Vauxhall 14 (XM 6747) and later a dark red open Vauxhall 23 hp. One year, this house was let and we rented 111 Gloucester Place (since renamed) and I can recall straw being put down in the street because a rich old lady opposite was ill and so the noise of the horses' hooves would be deadened. When my grandfather died in 1924, Papa clearly became richer and engaged a chauffeur called Whaley and we had a wonderful old Rolls Phantom, which also had the great merit of taking trunks on the top so that we could save the railway fares and drive up in it to Carlton, taking seven or eight hours, for the maximum speed was 55–60. Later this was sold and a more modern Rolls purchased, which lasted till the war.

We used to walk to Hyde Park and back each morning and afternoon with the younger children in prams or a 'mail cart'. We played at the back of the bandstand rather than the daisy walk which was too smart. Annie wisely said we were not to get too muddy when we played because of all the dogs and other filth. She used to explain Carlton dirt was clean dirt but London dirt was dirty dirt!

My father moved to 42 Pont Street where Mark was born and I can remember I bicycled to London, taking 33 hours after sleeping 9 hours at John Jefferson's aunt's house at Newark. The third one in the party was Michael Fogarty who got a classics scholarship to Christ Church at Oxford and is now a Professor of Economics at a Welsh university.

After the Second World War, Papa sold the lease on 42 Pont Street and bought one for 23 Lennox Gardens. The family carried most of the furniture from 42 Pont Street to 23 Lennox Gardens to save having to hire furniture vans. Papa bought the lease for this house for £3,000 and a ground rent of £20 per year. It ran out before he and Mama died in 1970-71 and Cluttons, representing Smith's Charity, allowed me to re-negotiate it for £1,000 a year rent till they died, which 50-fold increase Papa felt a bad bargain!

We went to some children's parties and I can recall a children's Xmas party at Norfolk House, Duke Bernard's residence in St James's Square, which was demolished in 1938.

Flowers were sent by post from Carlton and the arum lilies were always packed by Nichols in cotton wool. Michael and I were first taught to read and write by Mary Gray, a farmer's daughter, in the open air under the big beech tree at Carlton. My mother had a passion for the open air, so we went to the open air school in Regent's Park and Gaveney House School, miles up the Finchley Road, beyond Swiss Cottage. We always travelled on the open top of buses. We never went into a cinema and the first film I ever saw was at Ampleforth.

Carlton was a farming village dependent on horses. In many of the far-off fields farm horses could be left for the night and the farm employees would bicycle back home so as to save the horses from the tiring trek back to the village. Most of these shelters have been demol-ished but one can still see the traces of the brick foundations. The village blacksmith, Holmes, worked next door to Hirds, the present grocer. The carts were made and the wheels repaired by Bob Hinsley, the carpenter at the bottom of the drive, opposite the Protestant Church. He was also the undertaker and I can recall him making elm coffins for the poorer villagers.

The toll bridge on the River Aire, built by the Stapletons, had been sold, but Carlton folk went over half-price. About 1930 the County Council built the present iron bridge. It was said that, with the tide flowing up the river, whooping-cough could be helped by breathing in the air. Both the Aire and the Ouse used to flood seriously until the War Agriculture Committee heightened the banks and installed the present electric pumps. Papa wisely got the boat out of the boat-house on the lake one low tide during a *very* bad flood lest it was jammed up against the roof. And as the flood got worse, we even rowed during a high tide round the Half Moon Wood.

We always had the village priest, called Father Duane, for Mass in The Towers on Fridays; he had a spaniel called Steve, named after the jockey Steve Donoghue. The parson, Mr Birks, lived at the Vicarage.

The First World War had little impact on the Carlton estate. Granny ploughed up the bottom of the park beyond Half Moon Wood and I can recall my mother keeping cockerels under the front door steps, which were as big as ostriches to me when I was just walking, two or three years old. I can well remember the Armistice Procession in the village which we watched looking through the old white, wooden gate at the bottom of the drive and there was one soldier marching in it. The direction was towards Selby. There was also a Peace Tea for the village children in the stable yard, but in the Second World War the house was turned into an Army hospital which never took in war-wounded. It was the overflow of the York military hospital. There were over 50 patients in the wards, which were the picture gallery, card room and Venetian drawing-room, which were all boarded up ten feet high. The state bedrooms were made into lavatories and bathrooms. The dining room became the nurses' and VADS' sitting-room and we ate in the harp room. My sisters became VADS and did the cooking, using the main kitchen and helped with the nursing. There was a resident RAMC doctor and, quite ridiculously, three or four firemen, living in the stables in case there was a fire. A mortuary, which is now the tractor shed, had to be built but was never used.

3
Ampleforth, Oxford and London

In 1924 Miles went to school at Ampleforth, about fifty miles north of Carlton. This was before the Benedictines had bought Gilling Castle as a preparatory school, so Miles, then aged nine, joined the preparatory school at Ampleforth itself, transferring three years later to St Oswald's in the Senior School. The head master of the day was the celebrated Father Paul Nevill. The only member of the present Ampleforth community who was Miles's contemporary and is still alive is Father Benet Perceval. The latter's charming sister Mrs Sara Rodger has long been the assistant librarian at Arundel.

In the course of writing this book I visited Ampleforth and had a long and very interesting talk with Father Benet, whom I had got to know when my own sons were at the school and he was Prior. He kindly wrote out some notes for me. I reproduce below his exact words concerning Miles.

Miles was a normal schoolboy – nothing exceptional either in studies or sport. Humble and matter of fact, always cheerful and keen to do well, became an under-officer in the O.T.C. – as it then was – and a great friend of its commanding officer, Fr. George Forbes, who later became a chaplain with the Brigade of Guards in the war. Made many life-long friends when in the school, especially among the monks, Fr. Paul Nevill, the Head Master, Fr. Stephen Marwood his housemaster, Fr. Durstan Poggi and Fr. Felix Hardy.

Miles was fortunate to be (eventually) in St Oswald's House whose housemaster was Fr. Stephen Marwood, a man with great influence. He was intimately concerned in every aspect of the school, was the Head Master's right-hand man and was considered by all to be a real man of God.

Later in life Fr. James Forbes, who became Master of St Benet's Hall, Oxford, became a constant friend and often acted as chaplain at Carlton.

Miles always regarded himself as essentially a soldier, not a banker, a duke or Earl Marshal, still less as the leading Catholic. As befitted a soldier, he spoke his mind simply and directly – and in the language of an Army officer.

At school he was especially interested in history and this became a lifelong interest. He read it at Oxford when he went to Christ Church, which he immensely enjoyed.

Father Basil Mawson and Father Mauras Powell were in charge of Junior House at this stage, and Miles settled in well. After just over a year however, he suffered a rather severe setback. There was a measles epidemic in the school and Miles had to have a mastoid operation in the old infirmary. This left him deaf in his left ear. It took him some time to recuperate fully and he had to drop back in his place at school after missing a term. Having recovered and got back as far as possible into the academic routine, he moved into the Lower School under Father Illtyd Williams and then into St Oswald's. He specialised in history, taught by Father Paul Nevill, supported by a lay master whom he considered an excellent teacher, Tom Charles Edwards.

He made friends easily but had two especially close companions: one was Peter (Father Benet) Perceval and the other was David Bailey who became Father Bede Bailey, for a period head of the English Dominicans and now the Order's archivist.

Miles was a good all-rounder at Ampleforth, working hard and taking a full part in sport without ever being a star. By his own admission he did not shine as a cricketer, playing only in what was called the Optimists' set. There were hints of a military future and taste for discipline in his becoming captain of shooting, an under-officer in the OTC and a school monitor. Also, in those days at Ampleforth, there was a lot of beagling and Miles was a keen participant. But perhaps his most memorable athletic feat was when he and a group of companions bicycled all the way to London at the end of the Easter term.

Miles left Ampleforth in 1933 having much enjoyed his time there. Three years before he left, new entrants to the school included the young George Hume, later to join the congregation taking the 'religious' name of Basil. He and Miles were to become lifelong friends and their lives became crucially intertwined in the years after 1975. It was in that year that Miles inherited his dukedom and in the following year the former Abbot of Ampleforth became Cardinal Archbishop of Westminster.

Living comparatively nearby, Miles subsequently made frequent visits to his old school. Father James Forbes, an Ampleforth connection, remained a close friend until he died as Master of St Benet's, the Benedictine House of Studies at Oxford. Father James's Memorial Requiem at the University Church of St Mary's, many years later, at which Miles of course was present, was attended by the whole of Oxford and was the first Mass celebrated there since the Reformation. It was a moving tribute to a great man, who had always been able to perceive greatness in others. He once said to me: 'I have never known anyone quite like Miles.' Miles, it may be added, was the chairman of many of the fund-raising campaigns for Ampleforth and Father James was the organiser. The school was a source of permanent influence for Miles. His two sons went there, as did numerous nephews.

Miles went up to Christ Church, Oxford, in the Michaelmas term of 1933 to read history. The Honours School of Modern History at Oxford comprised a period beginning with Julius Caesar's invasion of Britain in 55 BC. In the Thirties, when Miles went up, it ended with the close of the Victorian era. Oxford University was not only proverbially 'the home of lost causes' but always gloried in living in the past. Its history dons at that time believed that anything that had happened after the nineteenth century was 'too recent to be taught with certainty'. It was only with the Second World War that the Modern History syllabus was daringly extended to take in the period up to 1918, which date was later advanced to 1939.

Scarcely any of the changes in Oxford life, which from the early Seventies quickly accelerated, had in any way affected the University in Miles's day. Christ Church was even slower than most other colleges to adapt itself to change. The College and its splendid Cathedral church were a self-contained world. In 1945 the Dean – a Canadian, John Lowe, who had arrived with rather unlucky timing in the summer of 1939 – preached a famous sermon in Christ Church Cathedral in gratitude for the successful close of hostilities. 'We must give thanks', he declared, 'for the termination of a war which has affected not only the University, but the entire world.'

Miles's lodgings during his first year were in Kilcanon and for his second year in Peckwater. His first tutorials at 'The House' – as his college was always called by its own members – were conducted (for Roman history) by J. N. L. Myers. From there he graduated, for the Anglo-Saxon and medieval periods, to J. C. Masterman, while his principal tutor was the eminent Professor Keith Feiling, one of Oxford's foremost history scholars, who made important contributions to the study of the seventeenth and eighteenth centuries.

Miles worked hard but – as he afterwards said himself – 'not all that hard'. This was not because he led a hectic social life, as did many of his generation who had not yet overcome the hangover from the colourful days of an earlier period. Then, as Evelyn Waugh was famously to write in *Brideshead Revisited*, Tom Quad had resounded almost nightly with 'the familiar sound of the English county classes baying for broken glass'.

Almost every Sunday Miles had lunch with Professor and Mrs de Zulueta in their house in north Oxford. The former was a distinguished don of the University at the time, and their son, (Sir) Philip de Zulueta, was to become, with his wife Marie Lou, very friendly with Miles and Anne later on.

Had the undergraduates of Miles's day suddenly become more serious and responsible than those of the post-First World War period? The answer must be no, if we remember the motion passed by the members of the Oxford Union (during Miles's time) that 'This House is resolved on no account to fight for King and Country'. No one knowing Oxford gave this episode a second thought but there was a theory that certain high-up members of the Nazi party took it with deadly seriousness.

Miles did not attend the debate, and never even became a member of the Union. Nor was he a member of any of the 'smart' clubs such as the Grid or the Bullingdon, or even the Christ Church dining club, Loders. This calls for a further word about the description given of Miles's 'extrovert' character in later years. In fact, and perhaps surprisingly, Miles was never a natural extrovert. He was then, and long remained, a naturally shy person. He was also a very modest one. This combination has paradoxical results. It can even be said that, in his basic character, he took after his father who was intensely shy. Indeed, before the war, it was Miles's younger brother Michael who was the most social and jolliest of the elder boys, while Miles was always considered quiet and serious. But his aversion in later years to self-importance of any kind made him into something of an extrovert despite himself. He made, moreover, a deliberate effort – which was very successful – to overcome his shyness.

He always dreaded and disliked pomposity in any form. He thus reacted to becoming a duke with exaggerated, sometimes almost unnatural, diffidence accompanied by self-deprecatory jokes so as not to be treated too deferentially or with excessive formality. It was almost, at first, as if his apparently outgoing behaviour were some kind of cover for the reluctance, born of shyness, for social esteem. He was always totally without 'side' – though justly proud of his family and its high responsibilities. Devoid of all affectations, he was unfailingly friendly and universally popular.

So in his first two years at Oxford Miles was not nearly as gregarious as he became in later life. He made many of his (mostly Catholic) friends at the Newman Society, connected with the Roman Catholic chaplaincy under the direction at that time of Monsignor Ronald Knox. In fact Miles spent his last year at Oxford in 'digs' at the Old Palace, where the chaplaincy was based. It was an old rambling house nearly opposite Christ Church, and there he and two other undergraduates spent a happy year under the same roof as the exceptional Ronnie whose lifelong friend he became. This experience was to have a lasting influence on his life, as we shall see.

Among the items in the big deed-box kindly lent to me by Anne Norfolk are two chunky books crammed with essays and notes by Miles from his days at Christ Church. They show a characteristically systematic approach and keen interest, with a quick eye for detail. He got a very adequate degree and could no doubt have got an even better one had he worked harder.

Apart from anything else, his mind was very much on other matters, not least the possibility of war, although he was, in principle, an optimist. He told me many years later that after the Munich pact was signed in 1938, he had a bet with a friend that there would be no war. But this was still in the future. He joined the Oxford OTC in 1934 and went to the RA Battery, as he had been advised to do, since, when it came to the annual camp, he and his fellow trainees were looked after by regular artillery regiments and so did not have to groom the horses. During the term they used to ride on Port Meadow. Camp was at Larkhill and Miles was later to write in his diary: 'I can well remember

galloping around with 18-pounder guns, changing from square formation to diamond formation. We had a least one terrible crash but it was
all the greatest fun.'

In his second year in the Oxford OTC he was transferred to the
Infantry Vickers Machine-Gun Company, thought appropriate as he
was destined for the Grenadiers. A further step nearer came in 1936
with the temporary attachment to the 1st Grenadiers at Pirbright. This
apparent conversion to military tastes somewhat conflicts with his
having told Professor de Zulueta, at lunch one Sunday, that his father
wanted him to go into the Army and his mother wanted him to go
into the City, but that he himself could not decide 'which would be
worse'.

None of this interfered with his private social and sporting life and
he was often in London, especially during the Season. He was aged
twenty when he came to my sister's coming-out party; my brother and
I were only allowed to be present before the dinner preceding the
dance, so I did not meet Miles properly until he came to us for a subsequent smaller gathering. I remember the occasion well because, in
typically generous fashion, he went out of his way to be friendly. His
manner with unimportant small boys such as myself was wholly natural and somehow involving. I got to know him much better when he
came to stay with us on subsequent occasions in Rutland. I was
helped, too, in not being shy with him by having been friendly, for as
long as I could remember, with his younger sisters Miriam and
Miranda. Miriam, being older, was chiefly my brother's friend, while
I became the devoted companion of Miranda, a few months younger
than myself.

The Howards' house at 42 Pont Street was tall, deep and narrow. It
seemed, when first going in, rather dark and cavernous, but giving
promise, somehow, of special adventure. Our chauffeur, Gray, would
drive us there with our nanny and we would be greeted by the parlour
maid, whose name was Richardson. She and the under parlour maid
always wore dark red uniforms, complete, of course, with the regulation
aprons and caps. A similar uniform was worn by the head housemaid,
Alice. The cook was called Coffey. I usually hated parties, but I always
looked forward to the ones at Pont Street, which were easily, for me, the
best fun and the most friendly, especially if Miles happened to be present
for at least part of the time.

Richardson, or her colleague, would escort us up to the drawing-room, a large L-shaped room on the first floor, where we would be greeted by Nanny Johnston, or, as there were so many Howard children, her assistant, Annie Ferguson. The latter's title of 'nurserymaid' belied the fact that to us she seemed quite old. She was a plump and very jolly lady with rosy cheeks, a ready smile, a Scottish accent, and one particularly prominent front tooth.

Jolliness and a gift for friendship were an immediately noticeable characteristic of all the members of the Fitzalan Howard family. This was famous for being unusually large and also for the fact that all the children's names began with an 'M'. This came about because the eldest child's name began with 'M', and it was decided to follow suit with all the others. Miles's father, Lord Howard, had wanted their eldest son to be called by one of his own names, but had been overruled in this by Mona. She, as I well remember, was a forceful lady who usually got her way, her gentle husband always being too nice to thwart her. Lady Beaumont had chosen Miles as it was a long-recurring name in the history of her own (the Stapleton) family. It had cropped up in generation after generation and had belonged to a man famous for being the first ever Garter Knight, Miles Stapleton, in the reign of Edward III. (This Sir Miles Stapleton was one of the miniature model figures of famous British characters that were sold at a shop well-known for such objects and ornaments in the Burlington Arcade.)

No less than seven brothers and sisters followed Miles into the world over the next twenty years, number one being Michael. His first wife was Jean Hamilton-Dalrymple, who had a daughter and later tragically died of polio. Michael subsequently married Meg Newman, a cousin of mine, and they had four sons and one daughter. Michael's third and present wife is Vita, the widow of Sir Mark Baring. Michael had an extremely distinguished career in the Scots Guards and became a major-general, Colonel of the Life Guards and, finally, Marshal of the Diplomatic Corps.

Next was Mariegold who married Jerry Jamieson, and they had two sons. Then came Martin, who also had a gallant career in the Grenadiers. After the war he married Bridget Keppel, and spent most of his life looking after the house and estate at Carlton. They had four daughters and a son. The fifth child was Miriam, later to marry Peregrine Hubbard, who started a boys' private school after leaving the

Navy. Sadly, Miriam died in a road accident when still comparatively young. They had two sons and a daughter. Miranda, the sixth child, married Christopher Emmet, who has since died. They had three daughters and a son. The two youngest members of the family are Mirabel and Mark. Mirabel married Bernard Kelly and they have a family of seven boys and one girl. Mark, married to Jacynth (born Lindsay), was a postwar Coldstream officer and later a director of Fleming's. They have two daughters.

My sister Maureen, brought up and sharing a governess with Mariegold, has often spoken of the fun they had during her many visits to Carlton. The Howards have always been a very united and extremely happy family. Despite a basically strict framework, there was always an atmosphere of fun, with endless pranks and games.

My sister, indeed, was practically a member of the family. She and Mariegold – all through the Thirties – had lessons together every day in Lord Howard's study at 42 Pont Street. The families had keys to both Cadogan Square and Lennox Gardens, both nearby, and went to one or other on most afternoons. Neighbours included the Sidneys in Lennox Gardens, the eldest son in the latter family being William, later Lord de Lisle, a brother officer in the Grenadiers with Miles.

One particularly memorable series of events at Carlton centred on 17 September 1936, when there were extensive celebrations for Miles's coming-of-age, though his actual birthday had been some two months earlier. On 17 September, a Thursday, there was a dinner and dance followed by fireworks for the tenants. Miles's father, despite his outwardly rather serious and austere demeanour, never lost a boyish enthusiasm for fireworks. He even let them off in the tiny garden behind their London house whenever there was an excuse for doing so, much to the exasperation of the neighbours.

Next day there was another dinner and dance, this time for the indoor staff. Then, on the Saturday, there was a tea party and conjuring performance for the children.

On Miles's actual birthday, 21 July, he had been given a party at the Lancashire house of his grandmother, Ethel Lady Beaumont. His presents included a cheque, a hunter, a Labrador retriever and a gun case. Miles got on very well with his father, Bernard, an exceptionally nice man, who was to have, purely through being his unaffected self, a profound influence on the whole family. His devout attachment to the Catholic Church had far-reaching effects on all of them. There was a family chapel at Carlton where Mass was often said by the parish priest from the village or a visiting priestly guest. Regular guests included such major figures from the pre-war era as Archbishop David Mathew and Monsignor Ronald Knox. Every evening the family, occasionally accompanied by friends, would congregate in the chapel before dinner to recite a communal rosary. This practice went on even after the war.

It would have been natural that so prominent a Catholic family should have been friendly with the Cardinal Archbishop of Westminster, but there was at that time (1937) a special reason why the Fitzalan Howards should have become friendly with the senior member of the Catholic hierarchy of England and Wales. The man in question was Cardinal Arthur Hinsley, Archbishop of Westminster from 1937 to 1943. He was himself a native of the village of Carlton, hard by Carlton Towers. The family had known Arthur Hinsley since his earliest days. Indeed Hinsley often spoke to certain close friends – all influential in their different ways in English Catholic life – of the importance to him personally of his friendship with the Fitzalan Howard family. The latter were equally appreciative of their friendship with him. Miles was to write the Cardinal a letter early in the war with the suggestion that he should be buried at Carlton (though in fact he was to be buried at Westminster Cathedral, see p. 48).

Miles's father, Bernard – 'Bar' – Howard was not only a gentle and lovable man but also a wise one. He had always been anxious, for example, that Miles should get something extra from his education at Ampleforth. He was particularly keen that Miles should learn Spanish and German, as well as being as taught at school the more conventional Latin and French, and felt that he would benefit from foreign travel in the holidays. The young Miles thus made several trips abroad, including two visits to Cologne. There, for a fortnight on each occasion, he came under the tutorial care of Dr Blussneck for his study of German. Though such expeditions are commonplace nowadays, they were by no means considered such before the war.

It should be added at this point that Bernard Howard, despite these enlightened initiatives, was an extremely shy, old-fashioned, and rather introverted individual. His shyness was partly a result of his having been seriously frightened of his bullying father. His stepmother, too –

his father had remarried – he found unsympathetic. He suffered from childhood from a pronounced stutter of which he was never able to cure himself. His closeness to all his children was partly due to a horror of ever inducing in them the sort of fear he had experienced at home.

The chief credit of being the enduring inspiration of a unique family, to which Miles was later to assume the role of successful 'pater familias', must go to Bernard Howard. He was himself a successful businessman whose City connections were the background to the family's later connection with Fleming's. He preceded and, almost always, followed his day's work in the City with a visit to church to pray – as 1938 moved into 1939 – that the 'peace with honour', however precarious, might somehow hold. Miles was now a soldier.

4

Prelude to War

This chapter is concerned with the short period between when Miles first joined the Brigade until soon after the outbreak of war, including, as it does, bits of information not included in Tony Chambers's account.

This comes about for several reasons. Although Miles wrote some notes later on the 1937–39 period, he did not start writing his diary, as such, with detailed descriptions of his Army service, until September 1939. Moreover, he did not record all his Army activities in the first year or so of the war. They were the subject, however, of one or two of those long conversations Miles and I had in St Kitts fifty years later, of which I took detailed notes as soon as our conversations had finished.

It was after three years of OTC work that Miles became a full soldier. This was in September 1937 when he joined the 1st Grenadiers at Wellington Barracks. Among the friends who joined at the same time were Neville Wigram from Oxford and Mervyn Sands. They all, including Miles, got an immediate sixteen-months' seniority because of their Oxbridge Honours degrees.

The authorities were conscious of public sensitivity about the possibility of war and although, by the spring of 1939, trenches were openly being dug in Hyde Park opposite Kensington Barracks, the atmosphere was quite different eighteen months earlier. Drilling took place out of sight of the public for two or three months under RSM Brand and Drill Sergeants Teese and Robinson. The Commanding Officers were, first, Arthur Wiggins, then Jack Aird, then Willie Fraser and, much later, John Prescott, who commanded the battalion at Dunkirk. Algy Heber Percy was the Adjutant, followed by Danny Dixon. The neighbouring battalion at Wellington Barracks was the 1st Coldstream, commanded by Oliver Leese. Miles was allotted Guardsman Paxton, who remained his soldier servant for most of the war with wonderful loyalty. His funeral service was at Brighton in November 1983, attended by Miles.

I remember Miles's speaking of Paxton many times. He was one of Miles's truest friends.

In January 1938 Miles became mortar officer but never went on a mortar course. They went on elaborate manoeuvres at Popham in the summer of 1938 and, later, both battalions moved to Chelsea Barracks. Miles got bored of changing guard and tried to become Assistant Military Attaché in Mexico but the application was not allowed by the Adjutant. He was selected instead to be ADC to Arthur Hope, Governor of Madras, but the War Office stopped able-bodied young subalterns taking such jobs.

In February 1939 Miles went on the small arms musketry course at Hythe, Kent with – among others – Basil Eugster, who was to become a lifelong friend. With Hitler claiming the Sudetenland as an excuse for grabbing Czechoslovakia, the British Plebiscite Force was formed, for which the 1st and 2nd Grenadiers were amalgamated into one war-strength battalion.

In June Hore-Belisha doubled the Territorial Army and the Brigade of Guards found twenty adjutants for the Territorial 2nd Battalions of those regiments whose home battalions were already out in Palestine, until officers could be sent back by sea. And so Miles was sent to start off the 6th Battalion Green Howards TA. His time was largely spent touring the North Yorkshire drill halls and giving instruction in the evening. Apart from anything else, he was delighted to be back in such familiar territory, near the scene of his happy days at Carlton.

As 1939 took its course, Miles became reconciled, along with practically everyone else in England, that war was now almost inevitable. There were at this time three battalions in the Grenadier Guards. Quite soon there were six. Soon after war was declared, Miles, with the 1st Battalion, went over to the Continent as part of a task force to bolster defences against an expected German attack. It was a task beset from the very beginning with formidable difficulties.

The Maginot Line protecting France from Germany was thought to be impregnable. It extended from Switzerland northwards only as far as there was an actual common frontier between France and Germany. Should Germany decide to direct its attack through the Low Countries, its army would meet a considerably more fragile fortification system.

One of the assignments of Miles and his fellow members of the BEF was to devise ways of strengthening the defences between the Low

Countries and Germany. These produced a series of comparatively light fortifications, largely consisting of a string of pill-boxes. Miles was among those charged with digging trenches to plug, as was hoped, the gaps between pill-boxes. But when the expected blitzkrieg was finally launched in the spring of 1940, and the 'phoney war' was over, the German Panzer division made short work of these precarious defences.

In 1940, while ostensibly at Staff College, Miles was seconded to a hush-hush special committee to discuss a strategy in case Spain should join the war on Hitler's side and Gibraltar be lost. This plan, of course, never had to be put into action.

The next part of the story, as far as Miles as a soldier was concerned, is vividly described in two chapters by Tony Chambers covering the periods 1937–49 and 1950–67. The intervening chapter, by the main author of the book, describes Miles's and Anne's romance and marriage.

PART TWO

Soldier

I

1937–1949

TONY CHAMBERS

Miles joined the 1st Battalion Grenadier Guards from the Oxford Officer Training Corps in August 1937. Drill at Pirbright was followed by the Small Arms School at Hythe. He had not been to Sandhurst and the School of Infantry did not exist until 1941. However, he had the good fortune to take part in the intensive divisional exercises 1938/9 under the new 3rd Division Commander, Bernard Montgomery, later the victor of El Alamein. Monty was fanatical about training, which in the event of war was to a great extent to make up for the deficiencies in equipment.

By September 1939 Miles was his battalion's anti-tank platoon commander with three 25mm Hotchkiss guns. It says something about the unreadiness of the Army to defend against German Panzer divisions, supported by ground attack Stukas, that three, as Miles described them, 'one pound pop guns' were the only anti-armour weapons for 800 crack infantry soldiers. The one big advantage for Miles was that the guns were drawn by Pick-Up carriers, so he and his platoon did not have to march. It should be remembered, whilst visualising the events to come, that the infantry then either went by boat, train or marched. The total miles marched by the 1st Battalion between 10 May and 1 June 1940 was 260.

When war was declared Miles went up to Carlton to take leave of his parents. Miles always described how his mother, never expecting to see him again, made the sign of the cross on his forehead, a practice continued afterwards by Miles with his own family. The only men who had survived the British Expeditionary Force in 1914 were the wounded and a few prisoners. That war had ended only twenty years before 1939, which is a shorter period than between now and the Falklands war.

The 1st Battalion formed, with 2nd Grenadiers and 1st Coldstream,

7th Guards Brigade; which with 8th Guards Brigade, 9th Infantry Brigade, a machine-gun battalion, a light tank regiment, a light artillery regiment and supporting troops made up Monty's 3rd Division.

They left Southampton on 29 September being made up of 60% regulars and 40% reservists. One Grenadier reservist, a London bus driver, had been so keen to rejoin that he abandoned his bus full of passengers in Sloane Street that Sunday morning (3 September) and despite the vocal complaints of his passengers legged it for Wellington Barracks. During a very wet autumn and extremely cold winter they dug in, forming part of the Gort Line in the village of Annappes on the Belgian border. The River Marcq provided a tank obstacle on the 1st Grenadier sector and they spent the whole winter digging an anti-tank ditch with bulldozers, back-trenchers and other mechanical diggers. As Miles wrote in his diary: 'This useless Line called the Gort line was apparently held for about two hours in the retreat back from Louvain. Lille was where we all went to shop and dine out. In November we went to Nantes to pick up our requisitioned British trade lorries. The Brigade anti-tank platoons formed a company, had its own mess, and was completely independent.' The company commander was Geoffrey Bull, who was later killed while gallantly trying to hold the Dunkirk perimeter commanding 4th Berkshires.

Miles's diary records: 'About this time I wrote to Cardinal Hinsley saying I was likely to be killed before he would die but I hoped he would be buried at Carlton. He most charmingly replied that he did not mind where he was buried. It turned out that a niece had him buried in Westminster Cathedral where his tomb is of no significance, whereas it would have been quite an exhibit in the Catholic church graveyard at Carlton!'

On 6 December King George VI inspected the anti-tank company, which marched past to the tune of 'Colonel Bogey'. In December Monty exercised them against an infantry tank battalion. After this Miles went back to Carlton for Christmas. In the New Year he tried to volunteer for skiing training in Canada for operations in Norway or Finland, but Bull dissuaded him:

I feel I must record how bored I am; it goes deep for, besides the gloom of immediate spurious activity, there is the realisation that ultimately we will all be killed on this front; so why go on waiting now? I feel very envious of those who have gone to Norway, where the fighting must be fun and the chances of survival are a reasonable gamble – anyhow better than those of a human unit here.

In March he went to Paris, got 'flu and went back on leave again to Carlton travelling with Billy Hartington, the Duke of Devonshire's heir, in the Coldstream, who appears again later. It should be remembered, when judging the BEF, that they had spent eight months in these extremely uncomfortable defensive positions. All to no avail as on 10 May 1940, when the Germans invaded Belgium, the brigade moved up to defend the River Dyle at Louvain. The problem was that the Belgians, whose fighting qualities were uncertain, insisted on defending the whole city, because of its historic importance, rather than the west bank, the Commanding Officer (J. A. Prescott)'s preferred position. Miles's guns were sited with the point company in the railway marshalling yards, a much inferior position against German armour. Both the river and canal were behind them and the bridges easy artillery targets, even if they weren't blown by their own side before they could get back. Miles dug gun pits and turned over some rail wagons to channel any advancing tanks into an enfilading target. As Miles explained to me and my children on the beach at Dunkirk when taking him skiing in 1978 on the way to the family visit to the Pope, 'Your best chance was to knock a track off or if you were very lucky hit the exhaust or the petrol tank. Everywhere else the stupid things bounced off.' This was the only time he spoke of these events to me.

The opening attack when it came was blitzkrieg-style, tanks and mounted infantry supported by Dorniers. For the twenty-four-year-old Miles, who had never seen action before, it must have been absolutely terrifying, the equivalent of opening your boxing career by going twelve rounds with Mike Tyson. The Belgians faded, the Grenadiers filled the gaps, held the railway station and counterattacked. Miles was mentioned in despatches. Monty's diary reads: '15 May. Enemy attacked on left of the RUR [Royal Ulster Rifles] front and got into Louvain station, counterattacked and pushed out (1000 hrs). At 1430 hrs attack developed on Coldstream front; heavy shelling all afternoon; Coldstream suffered severe casualties but front intact.'

It was during this engagement that a colleague, Jerry Seymour, was wounded, inspiring Miles's quip, 'Don't worry, Jerry, that's not blood, it's port.' Guardsman Cobsham had gone back for him, winning the MM. Four hundred German prisoners were taken, some of whom when they got back to the beach were instructed by the drill sergeant in the 'Eyes right', before marching past General Alexander, who took the salute.

Monty was supremely confident in the division that he had trained. He was arguably the best training officer the Army has ever had, particularly when you consider the paucity of the equipment and transport. As he described it, 'the division was like a piece of steel'. From dawn he spent all day with the forward units and went to bed early. One staff officer, who awoke him with news that the Germans had got into Louvain, was amazed to be told 'Go away and don't bother me. Tell the Brigadier in Louvain [Beckwith-Smith] to throw them out.' With the Belgians gone, the brigade was withdrawn to the west bank of the Dyle. The Germans tried to cross opposite the Coldstream. Brigadier James Langley describes how over-confident they were, driving up to the canal in full view of his observation post in a farmhouse roof, unloading rubber boats and beginning to inflate them. Langley describes how sickened he was to order his two leading sections, dug in on the bank, to open fire.

During the attack David Bonsor, Miles's equivalent in the 2nd Grenadiers, was wounded. 'I found a wheelbarrow and wheeled David to an ambulance and took away the breech of the gun. Our sixty pounders came into action and annihilated a school on the horizon: I felt we were invincible and would soon advance towards Berlin and was amazed when Regimental Sergeant Major Sheather told me that we were in fact about to withdraw.'

The Dyle line held and no one could believe it when they were ordered to withdraw behind the Escaut Canal, lest they be surrounded, following the Belgian and Dutch surrender on the left and the rout of the French 7th Army on the right.

17th May we pulled out by night and gradually retired to successive positions on the River Dendre and River Scheldt etc. We saw a Leander shot down by Messerschmitts. We made gun positions out of houses and, I regret to say, ate the food and wine we found in the larders and cellars. And we used furniture such as chairs etc., to make the gun positions more comfortable.

There were endless rumours of spies and I was nearly shot once
when I said in the dark to an English sentry: 'Je suis un officier
Anglais', thinking he was a Frenchman. There were long drives in
the dark and the battalions were marching back. We kept on being
bombed and machine-gunned by many Heinkels. I think we withdrew from Louvain on 17 May (night) to the River Dendre; to the
River Scheldt on 19th May with 1st and 2nd Grenadiers and on
the right, 3rd Grenadiers – the left flank of 1st Division. [The first
time in history all three Grenadier battalions had been in the line
together.]

His diary summarises:

    1. 18 May – Awake all night
    2. 19 May – Awake till three. Sleep till 7.
    3. 20 May – Awake till three. Sleep till 7.
    4. 21 May – Awake all night.
    5. 22 May – Awake all night.
    6. 23 May – Asleep.

It was a brilliant withdrawal (the most difficult phase of war) which
the division had practised several times in training, thanks to Monty's
prescience. The 1st Battalion arrived exhausted on the Escaut between
Oudenarde and Manucle, but very well fed. The quartermaster had sent
the Battalion butchers into the deserted farms. Considering the rest of
the BEF were on half rations, this was a great tribute to the efficiency of
the Grenadier family system. It was here that the 3rd Grenadiers under
Allan Adair were ordered to counterattack across the canal, an incred-
ibly successful action which held up the German advance for four vital
days and in which Lance Corporal Nicholls won the first VC of the war.
    General Brooke (later Field Marshal Viscount Alanbrooke) decided
to hold the Ypres-Commines Canal to form the Dunkirk perimeter. The
3rd Division was ordered to hold the Furnes sector at all costs, and
these were high – including 2nd Grenadiers Commanding Officer and
three company commanders. On the perimeter Miles's platoon formed
part of a brigade anti-tank company, the leading edge of the perimeter
defence with Brian Horrocks's 9th Middlesex Divisional Machine-Gun
Battalion. Note how so many key players in the war to come, Brooke,
Montgomery, Alexander, Horrocks, Adair, were all there.

Miles dug in his three 'one pounders' facing General Bock's Panzer Corps with every prospect of being killed, wounded or taken prisoner. The anti-tank companies would be the last to leave, if at all. Miles spent from 28 May to 1 June in this position. During the night of 1/2 June the Brigade was ordered to slip out of the line and pass through a French division. Sir John Nelson, from whom Miles and Anne bought a house thirty-seven years later, describes in his book: 'At 01.30 we reached the French division thinly dug in on the last line of defence. As we halted to be checked through I, rather anxiously, asked the Colonel commanding there how long he anticipated holding on. "Pour toujours" he replied and, to the undying credit of those gallant Frenchmen, he was as good as his word.'

On arrival at the beach the Battalion marched past General Alexander and formed up on parade, under fire. This cool demonstration of Guards' discipline inspired great confidence in the confusion. Miles told me, on the actual beach itself, that at the end of the parade the Commanding Officer thanked the Battalion for its outstanding performance and said that sadly they could not go back as a battalion, nor by companies nor even platoons, but that each section was to make its own way using its own initiative and God willing they would all meet up at Pirbright the day after tomorrow. The parade was then dismissed and Miles told me of his tremendous sense of isolation. He sent off his sections to the waiting queues and waited with three others to bury the breeches at low tide. By then it was the late afternoon of the 2nd and he and the others made their way along the Mole, the breakwater at Dunkirk. This was a slow and nerve-racking business, not only under constant artillery and dive-bomb attacks, but there were several gaps which were covered by loose boards. Miles had the good fortune to get on a Royal Navy trawler (HMS *Venomous*) after about six hours, to be greeted by a white-coated steward who gave him a pint of beer and a copy of the *Evening Standard*. A French officer with him was so impressed that he recalled 'Zair were bims all over ze boat and I vos given a visky and zoda. Zen I knew ze British could never lose ze war.'

Miles's diary records:

1st June – We deployed our guns on the beach in case there was a tank attack and there was continual shelling and air battles. We saw the battalion form up on the promenade in good order like

Wellington Barracks before being dismissed to re-form in England. We scuttled our guns by letting the tide come in over them. Henry Green, Gdsn Paxton, my orderly, and I decided to go along the Mole where the crowd eventually moved forward whenever a boat came in. A Margate steamer came in and we moved nearer, then a naval boat, which turned out to be HMS *Venomous*, came in, on to which we scrambled and officers were ordered to go to the Wardroom. We landed at Dover where I rang Carlton and went to Twesledown Camp, Aldershot: I went over and had a bath with my brother Michael at Sandhurst and slept for 24 to 30 hours.

Miles got his Mention, but Colonel John Prescott refused to put any of the 1st Grenadiers in for medals, saying no one had done more than their duty. Colonel Arnold Cazenove, on the other hand, put in many Coldstream officers and got a DSO himself. There was considerable feeling about this.

The 3rd Division was quickly reorganised, brought up to strength, and was at Frome, the first division to be re-equipped to be sent back to France. Then Pétain surrendered and plans were made to send it to the Azores and then Southern Ireland! Monty was furious with both the changes of plans and their innate craziness. There was no leave, which was particularly harsh on the men, whose families often did not know that they had got back. Most homes did not have telephones and the lines, in any case, were reserved for war traffic.

On 20 June the Division was sent to defend the Sussex coast and the 1st Battalion found itself at Brighton. Churchill's diary note reads: 'I was amused to see a platoon of the 1st Battalion Grenadier Guards making a sandbag machine-gun post in one of the kiosks on the pier, like those in my childhood where I had often admired the antics of the performing fleas.'

Miles was made adjutant and moved to Whiteways Lodge, Arundel. 'I had dinner with John Prescott and Bernard [Norfolk] in the smoking room. My first visit to Arundel, but not my last!'

A reasonably pleasant summer was passed on the south coast. A Grenadier officer recalls:

The only moment when the heart beats any faster is just before dawn, when we take out our patrols through the sleepy country-side. We are ordered to watch for dropping parachutes, winking lights, 'suspicious-looking' people – any civilian astir at that hour therefore becomes suspect – but, though we have drawn a blank so far, we come back to our breakfasts wet with dew from the orchards and the corn, and glowing with a sense of duty well performed.

The only excitement was on 7 September when barges were seen moving to Ostend and Le Havre. The code word 'Cromwell' (invasion imminent) was issued, everyone stood to, the Home Guard was called out and the church bells rung. One Grenadier company commander recalls: 'I went round the billets, doubled the sentries, released the men in arrest and ordered the drummer to sound the alarm. Our country buses purred quietly in a field, their civilian drivers talking quietly to the guardsmen drinking cups of tea. Then, for there was nothing else to do, we wrote our last letters and waited.' Ten days after this invasion scare, the Germans postponed 'Sealion' indefinitely because they had lost air supremacy, their plans were extensively known to the British and with the readiness of the Home Fleet to repel the landing, they had little hope of obtaining naval superiority. After the war General Jodl commented: 'Our arrangements were much the same as Julius Caesar's.'

Miles's diary records: 'Codeword CROMWELL was sent out and everyone stood to. The church bells rang except for the 1st Grenadiers because Sandy Vereker, Picquet Officer, had not understood it and I only learned next morning in the Orderly Room when we were told to stand down.'

Things were looking better and Miles was told he would be sent to the Staff College in the New Year, following a recommendation by Monty who had asked for all the names of officers who had served him in May and who were suited to staff training, regardless of their rank, following the exemplary action from the Dyle to Dunkirk. 'I would like to thank all officers and men for the way in which they have striven to increase the fighting efficiency of the Division; it is their efforts, and not mine, which enabled the Division to "see off" the Germans so successfully.'

The thing that inspired Monty, which was to affect Miles's career, was his (Monty's) view as to the need for the cavalry units under his command to cooperate fully with the infantry, which was left particularly exposed at night. This led to the formation of the Guards Armoured Division in November 1941.

In November the Battalion moved to Swanage, where it experienced some internal turbulence, which for Miles, as adjutant in charge of discipline, could have affected his career. His diary records:

> February 1941, Col. John Prescott went back to Birdcage Walk to command the Regiment and Col. Willie Goschen came and was hopelessly demanding.
>
> I went on a 48-hour leave and on my return found the battalion out on the streets, demanding Col. John should come back and Col. Willie should leave. Fortunately it rained so the disturbance ended. It was in fact really led by the company commanders. Brig. Arnold Cazenove said I was to be changed, so I reported back to Birdcage Walk to Col. John Prescott and explained the situation. The Major-General said I was in no way to be removed, so I returned to Swanage and Julian Gascoigne took over the battalion.

This relationship between commanding officer and adjutant, who share the same office, formed the basis of a crucial lifelong friendship.

In March 1941 Miles was posted as staff captain to a Dorset brigade, his first staff and extra-regimental job. Leaves were spent at Carlton. Amusingly the bulk of his regimental file is taken up with correspondence to various regimental adjutants, trying to cadge extra petrol coupons to get up to Carlton.

In October he went to the Staff College as a student until March 1942 when he took over HQ Squadron of Guards Armoured Division, with Patrick O'Donovan as troop leader of the Irish Guards troop. Miles was then made the divisional Deputy Assistant Adjutant and Quartermaster General, effectively the discipline, supply and administration officer. It was a mark of the esteem in which Miles was regarded that without any previous experience he was to run the supply and administration of an armoured division having been an infantry platoon commander less than two years before. Armoured divisions are much more complex to supply than the infantry, requiring tons of fuel, ammunition, spare parts etc. Even when the enemy is not involved, tanks are notoriously unreliable and require constant attention. This also applied to the signals equipment. It would have been difficult enough had he had any direct experience, but it was an exceptional challenge and they did not know that they would not be sent to North Africa and into battle. Oliver Leese, the Divisional Commander, insisted that all officers learnt all the skills. Leading by example, he and his three brigadiers learned how to drive, fire and maintain tanks. Miles was sent to the tank gunnery school at Bovingdon. In September the Division assembled on Salisbury Plain with 5th Guards Armoured Brigade (Miles was later to be brigade major) and 6th Guards Armoured Brigade with which, in its later independent role, Michael, his brother, was to win the MC as a squadron commander.

Based at Red Lynch House near Wincanton, there then followed a year's intensive training on Salisbury Plain to get the infantry guardsmen up to speed as first-class tank crews. Miles was himself hard worked to keep these exercises administered and to see for himself all the problems, even without the interdiction of enemy fire.

In October 1942 he was posted as DAA and QMG of 24 Guards Brigade, where again he was in a spot of bother. His diary reads:

> Henry Green is Brigade Major and Dick Colvin the Brigadier. Only these knew the secret plan, which was covered in the Ops. room by three sacks on the wall. I guessed it was Tangier because Spain might come into the war and told Col. Guy Rasch, the Brigade umpire. Dick Colvin had me up and threatened me with court martial for guessing a secret, which was just as heinous as letting it out as having known it.

Miles went to 20 Beach Group as DAA and QMG, which was training to do a landing somewhere. They were sent up to Scotland to train: 'There were no rations on the train so at Doncaster I requisitioned the station restaurant and fed the whole train, signing it M. Howard 68110 Major and heard no more about it.'

On 10 April 1943 Miles and his faithful orderly, Guardsman Paxton, embarked from Liverpool for Algiers to prepare for the invasion of Sicily (operation Husky). Delays were caused by deep strategic differences between the US and the UK on the importance of Italy and the huge logistical difficulties of the first seaborne landing against an entrenched enemy since Gallipoli, which, as Churchill's responsibility, had been a spectacular failure with huge losses. It was a paradox that with Churchill's horror of seaborne landings the Italian campaign involved three such efforts, the last of which, at Anzio, was very nearly a costly failure.

They embarked at Sfax and landed the 51st Highland Division at

Capo Pachino and a severe battle ensued outside Catania. Miles had planned the landing with a young Sapper officer called Denis Healey. The future Chancellor and future Duke got on like a house on fire and a close relationship was formed which was not only a lot of fun, both being great characters, but valuable later in the House of Lords.

In Sicily, Miles was posted, as brigade major, to the 4th Armoured Brigade (commanded by the redoubtable Brigadier John Currie, DSO and two bars and MC), part of the 7th Desert Rats Division with the 8th Army. This was a very exciting appointment for Miles but fraught with difficulties because he was the new boy and, worse, from the Infantry, in a battle-hardened armoured brigade which had distinguished itself throughout the North Africa Campaign and most recently at Alam Halfa and El Alamein. When Rommel attacked on 31 August the brigade had made a distinguished counterattack on the southern flank of the Germans and had to be withdrawn because it was in danger of annihilation. During the two weeks of El Alamein, it cut off Rommel from his supplies, occupied his landing zones and destroyed enemy aircraft. Miles, on the other hand, had never been in a tank in battle in his life.

Tank casualties are particularly unpleasant as, if the machine is hit, and it probably catches fire, the whole crew can be burned or killed. Whereas in the infantry you spread out, so if one is hit it does not necessarily involve anyone else. In addition our tanks were inferior and the old adage that the best anti-tank weapon is a tank did not apply. The 88 gun used on German tanks and in their artillery was much superior. Our field artillery using the 25-pounder had no anti-tank capability.

'From the beginning', Miles told me, 'they treated me with a great deal of suspicion, watching what I would do on coming under fire. The thing was to keep standing and pay no attention.' They clearly had not heard of Louvain. But Miles's infectious character, wonderful sense of humour and huge administrative ability soon won them over and so he joined the victorious 8th Army, which justifiably saw itself as vastly superior to the rest of the Army. Miles's diary reads:

At first, he [Currie] tried to sack me because he wanted Major Harry Llewellyn. There was much shelling from the toe of Italy and when Brigadier John saw I could take it, he began to like and trust me. We fought around Etna on a one tank front. Finally the

enemy withdrew to the mainland and we received orders to repre-
sent 8th Army, linking with the Americans under General Patton.
General Patton arrived with an American Military Police escort,
motor bikes, white painted helmets etc. Since we were cut off, we
had very little except our khaki drill, which we had cleaned up
and General Patton, with great show of bombast, said how
pleased he was to link up; when Brigadier Currie, wearing his
faded red hat, which had become pink with the desert sun,
mentioned he had come from Alamein and the fighting had indeed
been hard in the desert. There was no question who dominated
this little conversation.

Fortunately, 4th Brigade was not in the van at the Messina crossing,
which was fiercely opposed by the Germans. The rather obvious problem of invading Sicily is that there are very few viable landing sites on
the adjacent coast.

Approximately September 1943 I swanned over to the toe of Italy
and returned to hear we were to embark for Taranto in LSTs etc.,
from Catania. We saw much of the Italian fleet sunk by the Fleet
Air Arm bombing at Taranto.

They advanced with very little opposition to capture Bari, Foggia,
(many airfields), Lucera, Serra Capriola, and San Savero. After leaving
Naples the army was bogged down at Monte Cassino and in order to
outflank the Germans an attack was made up the Adriatic coast. In
December they reached the Sangro, a major obstacle in full autumnal
spate. The most interesting thing about Miles's MC is that it was
awarded whilst he was a staff officer. Except in cases where divisional
headquarters were overrun particularly by the Japanese in Burma, this
is most unusual and happened as follows.
   The idea was to get the 4th Light Armoured Brigade across the river
to form the necessary bridgehead before the bridges could be built. The
situation was too tenuous for the Sappers to raft them across and suitable entry and exit points needed to be recce'd to enable the tanks to
swim. Recce patrols are an infantry duty and the brigade only had one
infantry regiment, the South Staffordshires, who had already suffered
severe casualties. The shortage of infantry officers was dramatic and
Miles told me that most of the platoons and even one company were

commanded by NCOs, due to excessively high officer casualties in Italy, a country which without exception suits defence. He therefore volunteered to Brigadier John Currie to go forward and lead a series of recce patrols across the river. The citation tells the rest of the story:

On 29th November 1943 during the battle of the River Sangro, Major Fitzalan Howard was Brigade Major at Tac Bde HQ. It was necessary for HQ to move at times up to the leading tps in very exposed positions and was subjected to sniping, shell and mortar fire. At all times Major Howard's coolness, cheerfulness and, above all, his infectious enthusiasm for the battle was an encouragement and example to all who came in contact with him. When the tanks were held up by mines and the operation was halted, Major Howard undertook several recces on foot and showed the greatest energy and coolness in complete disregard for the enemy fire spreading cheer and optimism wherever he went.

The lovely thing is that he won it in such a characteristic manner – 'infectious enthusiasm', 'encouragement and example to all who came in contact with him', perfectly summarising his very endearing qualities. Miles's diary describes it:

I patrolled by night to see if Sherman tanks could ford and I mentioned to Brigadier John that my 'privates' had just got wet and it was concluded that Sherman tanks could easily wade up to that depth. We had a terrific battle; and on the other bank we were being shelled by an Indian Field Battery, which I succeeded in stopping by running to the Field Regiment Command Tank etc. I got my Military Cross for all this.

He then adds: '25th December – Xmas. Midnight Mass in Oliver Woods' Squadron Mess said by Father Topsy at Fossacesia.'

Miles's luck held and soon afterwards in the New Year he sadly took leave of Brigadier Currie, a brilliant Gunner commander of a cavalry brigade who had taught him all he knew about tank tactics. In addition he learned the invaluable lesson that armoured brigades had far too little infantry and it was this lesson that when eventually applied to the Guards Armoured Division led to its success.

Whenever Miles mentioned Currie he never failed to say how much he liked and admired the man who took his brigade from Alamein to the Sangro. It must be remembered that 8th Army casualties, prisoners, and indeed postings meant that only about 5% of units to cross the start line at Alamein reached the Po valley. Currie himself was sadly killed still commanding 4th Brigade in Normandy. He is buried in the Bayeux cemetery. 'Evy Hambro later told me John Currie had ordered him to write out a recommendation for my MC after the Sangro. After our return Evy Hambro married Mary Lyon from Wentbridge near Carlton, and I was best man.'

What people forget about the Second World War is that the battles were just as bad as the First War but there were fewer of them, with long interludes for the individual – e.g., for Miles, June 1940 to July 1943.

In March 1944, after embarkation leave, Miles was compulsorily exchanged by Montgomery to be brigade major of 5th Guards Armoured Brigade commanded by Brigadier N. W. Gwatkin, consisting of 1st (Motor) Battalion Grenadier Guards and three armoured battalions, 2nd Grenadiers, 1st Coldstream and 2nd Irish Guards. Martin, Miles's younger brother, was a tank troop commander in the 2nd Grenadiers. This must have given Miles particular anxiety when the battle was joined.

They trained around Helmsley, and were inspected by the King at Duncombe Park. These were the slightly lyrical spring days with Sunday Masses at Ampleforth described in Hugh Dormer's[1] diary. Miles was however not happy, feeling bypassed in the chain of command and being much resented for his battlefield experience. 'I carefully kept quiet and did not boast any battlefield experience, even though they needed it.' The Division which had trained for two and a half years under Allan Adair moved down to the Brighton/Eastbourne area at the end of April. The Guards Division was landed on D plus 18, with the advantage of being all brother regiments, both armoured and motorised infantry ready to support each other at all times, including at night, in stark contrast to the experiences of 1940. Miles's diary reads: 'It became wonderfully efficient. Never have infantry been better supported. There was no nonsense of tanks withdrawing at night to refuel and re-arm, leaving the infantry naked all night without tank support.' However, things did not get off to a very good start when they

---

1 S.O.E. with the Maquis in France and Squadron Leader Irish Guards in Normandy.

anchored off the Mulberry harbour in a storm and spent five days in extreme discomfort before being able to disembark.

Operation Goodwood, the major attack east of Caen, began on 18 July. The diary states: 'We advanced by night with searchlights shining off the clouds; reflecting down on the terrain. It was only a limited advance – as said by Monty when he briefed us – to attract 14 German divisions, so that the Americans had only three divisions opposite them when they broke out; and later bottled up the Germans in the Falaise pocket when the air forces destroyed so many of them.'

At 6 a.m. Miles's brigade led the approach march to the bridges over the Orne. Most unfortunately an 88 ack-ack battery was brought into an anti-tank role, such was the super-efficiency of the Germans having one all-purpose gun. Within minutes sixteen tanks were ablaze and by the end of the day the Division was reduced to less than half their tanks. It was in this engagement that Hugh Dormer was killed. The awful truth is that the enemy had anticipated 5 Brigade's thrust south east of Caen and were ready for them. Every advantage lay with the defenders, the ground haze was thickened by the dust, churned up by the armour, and dense hedges and belts of tall trees limited the vision of the tank commanders. The 2nd Grenadiers' leading squadron lost its commander and two troop leaders. Martin, the No. 3 Troop leader, survived this, his first engagement and it is difficult to imagine a worse baptism of fire. Peter Carrington, the second in command, and Martin were the only squadron officers to come through. Miles must have been worried sick and despatched the King's Company to be under the command of Rodney Moore, the 2nd Grenadiers' Commanding Officer. The motorised infantry were then able to get into Caen and clear it for the tanks.

The whole thing had been thoroughly confusing and was not a promising start. Cromwell shells bounced off the German Tiger tanks whilst the Shermans easily caught fire, so that the Germans aptly nicknamed them the 'Tommy cookers'. However, the British tanks were much more mobile than the Tiger and we had more fuel and more tanks. At one point the inferiority of the British tank guns led some tank commanders to simply ram the Tigers. Sixty-eight tanks were reported missing but by daylight more had limped in. The casualties were not as bad as originally thought – 330, of whom 79 were killed including the Commanding Officer of the 1st Welsh Guards and his successor the following night, with the CO of the 5th Coldstream wounded in both legs. Although the attack had enabled the Americans to break out, lessons needed to be learned and it was very much Miles who pointed out that for obvious reasons the infantry brigade had not been able to keep up with the armoured brigade. It was essential that the Infantry were in a position to clear the 88 emplacements. The 88 was vulnerable to a creeping barrage in front of an infantry attack and RAF ground attack fighters. This is well illustrated in the film *A Bridge Too Far*.

The Division was therefore regrouped in line with Miles's original thinking. Instead of confining almost all the armour to one brigade and the motorised infantry to the other, each brigade had two groups of one tank and one motorised infantry battalion from the same regiment. This gave the triple advantage of a square balance (tanks/infantry), the ability of the infantry to keep up, and full cooperation between brother battalions.

Miles's brigade was then engaged against the best SS troops in the Caumont area. They hung on to a very isolated position for four days at La Marvindiere during which they were counterattacked several times and it was very difficult to get supplies up to them or casualties away. The occupation of this key point prevented the enemy re-establishing his front and loosened up the whole position, developing into the Falaise trap.

Meanwhile, a few miles south of Caumont, Michael and Martin Fitzalan Howard unbeknown to each other, were engaged in the same battle. At 0930 on 6 August, No. 2 Squadron, 2nd Grenadiers (Martin was in No. 1 Squadron), which was the tank regiment in the Grenadier group in Miles's brigade, was ordered to take Estry with the Gordon Highlanders. No one knew that the Germans had been ordered to defend Estry to the last man, as it blocked the road to Falaise, cutting the Germans off in the Caen encirclement. The plan was for Michael, commanding his Churchill Tank Squadron in 3rd Scots Guards (containing two other future generals, the future Archbishop of Canterbury, Robert Runcie, and the future Deputy Prime Minster, Willie Whitelaw), to pass through the Grenadiers and Gordons and capture Le Theil. But the Germans intended to hold Estry at all costs with minefields, anti-tank guns, Panther tanks, and 88s. By 1615 the situation had become desperate for the Grenadiers and Gordons with incessant

infantry and tank casualties. Michael and the HLI were kept back. At 7
o'clock it was decided that what was left of No. 2 Squadron Grenadiers
would withdraw and Michael and the HLI were ordered to make a final
attempt on the Estry crossroads, where the Gordons were still holding.
The infantry, held up by machine-gun nests, directed the fire of the
tanks and silenced the machine-gun posts. One officer hit a Panther
which replied setting his tank on fire. Lieutenant Bruce shot a German
officer, who was asking for his surrender, with a pistol. Michael's MC
citation takes up the story.

> The advance was extremely hotly contested by dug-in infantry,
> tanks and self-propelled guns and mortars and the infantry
> encountered very stiff opposition. Major Fitzalan Howard
> however maintained his squadron in the closest possible support
> of them in spite of the extremely difficulty going and together they
> managed to get into and secure the main cross road at Estry. These
> positions were maintained by the infantry and tanks under
> extremely heavy shell fire until the tanks were called back to
> forward rally next morning. The Officer Commanding H.L.I.
> himself told me that Major Fitzalan Howard's Squadron had
> given him magnificent support and that without it he would never
> have got on.

As light faded Michael's squadron formed a hedgehog protected by
and in turn protecting the remnants of the HLI and Gordons, where
they stayed under heavy mortar and machine-gun fire until 3 o'clock
the next day, 7 August, when the Brigadier ordered a withdrawal to
Montcharivel. 'The forming up for this move was personally directed
under intense mortar fire by the Squadron Leader, Major Fitzalan
Howard.'

As a result of the unforeseen hold-up at Estry, the Grenadier group
did not attack until 11 August, No. 2 Squadron having been severely
depleted on 6 August. Martin's No. 1 Squadron took the lead with 1st
Motorised Grenadiers. Martin had survived Goodwood and Caumont.
Here he was to lead the attack on Viessoix just past Estry. The
squadron was split into two, with Peter Carrington, commanding a
force to take the bridge, losing two tanks to mines and one to a
bazooka. Meanwhile, Captain H. F. Stanley with Martin's troop and
the 1st Grenadier Mortars got into Viessoix to meet the German 5th

Parachute Regiment, who fought with skill and determination and used the terrain to their best advantage to close in on the tanks with bazookas. Martin's tank was hit and he was wounded, whilst Lieutenant Misa was killed in his Sherman. 'During the engagement the enemy flagrantly breached the rules of war. A German ambulance, not fired at, drove within 10 yards of Lieutenant Kelso's tank and ten desperados leapt out hitting his tank with a bazooka and killing the troop leader with a grenade.' Martin was back in the battle by November, and later joined the Parachute Regiment, serving in the Palestine emergency 1945–47.

The diary records:

My brother Martin had been severely burnt on his hand and face when his tank blew up in Normandy. I just missed seeing him when I went back to the advanced dressing station but was shown a column of ambulances in which he was. He went to Wolverhampton and had skin grafts and returned to the 2nd Battalion. He then ran the Mess at Siegburg in the house of the 4711 Eau de Cologne German magnate! After V.E. day, he became a parachutist so as to get to see the war in Japan, but only got as far as Palestine.

Meanwhile, on the very same day, Michael was engaged less than five miles away. The second part of his MC citation reads:

On the 11th August he was ordered to support a company of 1st Welsh Guards in an attack on the important German OP on the spur running NE from Chenedolle. Owing to a series of deep ravines the tank going was extremely bad and direction difficult to maintain. In spite of this and some enemy opposition Major Fitzalan Howard drove his tanks forward with such determination that they dominated the ridge and permitted the Infantry to capture the spur with very little trouble.

In both these actions there is no doubt that Major Fitzalan Howard's cool leadership and undefeatable determination contributed more than any other single factor to the successful obtaining of those two objectives in the face of most difficult conditions and heavy enemy opposition and fire.

Shortly after, Michael was posted as Brigade Major 32nd Brigade, alongside Miles's brigade, forming Guards Armoured Division. Without any respite, he found himself as the chief staff officer of an armoured brigade about to advance hundreds of miles a day, responsible for planning all the complexities that that entails.

Once the Seine was crossed, Miles's brigade came under 30 Corps and things moved fast. The brigade now consisted of the Grenadier and Coldstream groups. From its inception the new organisation was an outstanding success as infantry/tank cooperation took on a new meaning; perfect trust was the keystone because the two battalions spoke the same language and the men knew each other well. Each company worked with the same squadron and each platoon the same troop. The division advanced 200 miles in two days and on 1 September drove into Arras. The French Resistance was an enormous help, taking over 3,000 prisoners and preventing the enemy destroying the bridges over the Somme at Amiens.

On 2 September they were given their next day's objectives – General Adair's great intention 'to advance and capture Brussels', seventy miles away. Miles's brigade was on the left with Michael's on the right. The race was on! The Grenadiers and Miles's brigade bumped into an enemy strong point consisting of eight anti-tank guns with infantry. The King's Company and 2 Squadron lost 22 killed and 31 wounded, clearing the guns. The race was on again with the Grenadiers ahead of the Welsh Guards, but they again came across more unexpected opposition and it was left to the Welsh Guards to be the first to liberate Brussels. It was an emotional and heady occasion with cheering crowds and girls kissing the guardsmen, and the very best champagne.

For the two brothers, apart from the day on which each won his MC, this must have been the most dramatic day of their lives. The competition between the two brigades, each with its fraternal brigade major, was so intense that Allan Adair had to decide on a winning post, the railway bridge in Brussels. Michael's brigade won.

... So it was left to the Welsh Guards Battle Group to be the first to liberate Brussels. Crowds of joyous, deliriously excited citizens barred the way, swarmed all over our tanks, screamed salutations to us, and pressed fruit and drink upon the tired, dusty, hot tank crews. German machine guns, anti-tank guns and snipers barked at us. We barked back, the crowds leapt off the tanks and dived into slit trenches and any other cover nearby. This gave the column some breathing space, and one was left wondering which was worse – to be kissed, hugged and screamed at by hysterical women while trying to give out orders over the wireless and to control the direction of your tank; or to be free of the crowd and shot at by Germans. The opposition was soon overpowered, and the crowds emerged excitedly and over-ran the tanks again. The last time I had been in Brussels was in July 1940, as a fugitive escaping from the Germans. On that occasion I had entered the city from the east in a tram. Today I entered it from the west in a tank.

The Guards Armoured Division had covered 250 miles in six days and was now to lead the advance.

After two days' celebration Miles's brigade liberated Louvain. It must have been very moving for Miles, whose anti-tank guns had held the railway yards in 1940, to go back as liberator in 1944. 'I sent the Grenadier Group on to Louvain because they (and I) had retreated from there in May 1940.'

The brigade was then ordered to capture Bourg Leopold after Michael's brigade had captured the Beeringen Bridge, over the Albert Canal. 5 Brigade was led by a Coldstream company commanded by Major Lord Hartington who had recently married Kathleen Kennedy. He was killed instantly while his only platoon commander, John Brabourne, the film director, who later married Patricia Mountbatten, was seriously wounded. This gallant action enabled 5th Brigade to reach the Escaut Canal, where the Irish Guards took the bridge intact with a Sapper officer calmly cutting the cables of the explosive charges. The machine-gun bullets were drumming into the wooden beams, but they worked steadily until they had removed the detonators from the charges in the piers. The success of capturing the Escaut Canal bridge had saved the 2nd Army several days, and enabled the date of the next advance to be brought forward. The bridge was immediately christened 'Joe's Bridge' – after the initials of the battalion commander, J. O. E. Vandeleur. General Horrocks came forward to congratulate the Group, and gave the Irish the doubtful honour of leading the next advance – Operation Market Garden, launched to take the famous 'bridge too far' at Arnhem.

Miles's brigade took over from Michael's, which had broken through to Eindhoven. This is the sequence in the film led by Michael Caine playing Joe Vandeleur. On 18 September the Grenadiers linked up with the US 82nd Airborne Division, who had been dropped too far from the bridge at Nijmegen. General Gavin, 82nd Commander, wrote: 'At almost our darkest hour the Guards Armoured Division, gallantly led by General Adair, came across the Maas and joined us... . I must say that in all my years in the war, I've never met such courage and gallantry and cooperation on the part of Allied troops as the Guards Armoured Division.'

Miles would have been in the background at the dramatic meeting between Norman Gwatkin, his brigadier, Adair, Horrocks the Corps Commander, Gavin, and Browning, commanding the three airborne divisions. A decision was made that the Grenadier group in Miles's brigade would go for the Nijmegen bridge. Casualties were appalling in getting to the bridge, but by 6 p.m. a troop of tanks, first tank Sergeant Robinson, second tank Lance Sergeant Parry, and third tank Peter Carrington, started over the bridge in the full expectation of being blown sky high. However, Sapper officer Tony Jones climbed across the girders and cut the wires under machine-gun fire. When Horrocks put him up for a VC he was turned down on the grounds that he was only doing his job! Horrocks was justifiably furious. This feat was so remarkable that the independent company of Grenadiers is now called Nijmegen Company. It was the most gallant of actions and matched by the unbelievable bravery of 82nd Airborne who paddled across the 400 yards of water in flimsy collapsible boats to take the railway bridge with 50% casualties.

The important thing to remember is that so much ground had been covered. It is difficult enough to make and implement plans (Miles's job) when you are static and almost impossible when you are constantly moving, with an ever-changing situation and continuously under fire. It was tactically brilliant but strategically disastrous, because the road between Nijmegen and Arnhem is built above a marsh so that it was easy to dig in the 88s and the Sherman tanks were sitting ducks, unable to leave the road without getting bogged down.

In 1981 I did a consultancy job for Amoco Chemicals at Nijmegen and our Belgian hosts took us out to lunch and we got talking about it. One of them, who had been sixteen at the time, said 'It was quite clear that this operation was never on.' In fact, as the Belgian explained, the Germans got in behind, and indeed Michael's brigade had to be sent back down the road to clear it. Monty and anybody who looked at a map could have known this in the first place. 'Theirs not to reason why...'

They spent the next two months resting, refitting and training. Allan Adair recalled: 'Some of us found relaxation in shooting (birds not Germans). I see from Michael Fitzalan Howard's Game Book that, with Brigadier Johnson, M. Gordon-Watson, T. F. Blackwell, Miles Fitzalan Howard and I, we shot fifteen partridges one afternoon during which it never stopped raining. We had a dog called Fizz which we bought off a German for a packet of cigarettes.' On 12 October the King visited them. In December Miles wrote:

I handed over Brigade Major to Savill Young. Monty had decided, very sensibly, to send about half a dozen Brigade Majors, including myself, back to the Staff College as instructors. I tried to persuade Monty to leave me but it was all to no avail and he only sent me one of his pamphlets on lessons of the campaign which I still have.

I was given a second mention in despatches for my efforts in the campaign. I left Brigade HQ in a jeep with Guardsman Paxton in the Sittard area with a lull on and Christmas in their thoughts. We deliberately visited my old Anti-Tank Platoon HQ in May 1940 at Louvain on the way back to Brussels and embarked at Ostend on an LST, landed at Tilbury and then to Fenchurch Street, where I read the papers to learn that the Battle of the Bulge by six German divisions had suddenly broken out.

The Commandant of the Staff College happened to be Major-General Philip Gregson-Ellis, to whose 3 Company, 1st Grenadiers I had been attached in August 1936 at Pirbright from Oxford. He was invited to witness the crossing of the Rhine and took me with him to see the bridge at Duisburg, so I think I was the first of Guards Armoured Division to cross the Rhine on 27th March 1945.

Miles was sent to teach at the Staff College at the age of twenty-nine, which at that time was for most the age of being a student. It was an extraordinary tribute to his staff skills and fighting experience. Most instructors were in their late thirties. 'I was an instructor at the Staff College with Brigadier Julian Gascoigne as Assistant Commandant. We ran a dance at Minley Manor, for which some RAF pilot students and myself got 500 bottles of champagne provided by the Eye Club of Guards Armoured Division in Brussels, smuggled into Blackbushe Airport.'

Meanwhile, Guards Armoured had reached the Elbe, met the Russians and it was all over. Since Normandy they had covered 1,500 miles with 956 killed, 545 missing and 3,946 wounded. In his tribute to the Division, Allan Adair wrote: 'Special mention must be made of the two Brigade Majors – the Fitzalan Howard brothers.'

Miles's diary concludes:

VE Day and I seriously considered (a) going into the City, (b) becoming an MP as John Hope did, or (c) transferring to the Foreign Office. This I discussed with Sir Eric Drummond. Special transfer terms were offered to those who had University degrees and who were born after 1 August 1915. But I missed this by having been born on the 21st July and so dropped the idea.

On leaving the Staff College in April 1945 Miles hankered after a job in Rome to see the new Europe unfold, but was then sent in April as a company commander with the 2nd Battalion in Lübeck. Miles had not served in a battalion for five years and the lieutenant-colonel (Dick Colvin) rightly decided he should get in some regimental service for the good of his career. (In the event Miles commanded three separate rifle companies in three different battalions.)

First he had to deal with the problems of the Lübeck black market. The temptations posed by the black market proved irresistible to some. It is a well-worn custom in the Regiment for a new company commander to attend pay parade for several weeks to learn the guardsmen's names. Oliver Lindsay records in *Once a Grenadier*:

But CSM White told me, to my surprise, that the men had not been paid for at least six months because, although it was not really allowed, each Guardsman received 50 cigarettes per week which they were selling for Reichsmarks on the black market, and with the Reichsmarks they were easily able to buy their allocation of 150 cigarettes from the NAAFl. The profit the Guardsmen made was put into the Post Office Savings Bank. I understand that the British Government lost about £80 million pounds before this practice was stopped. The officers did not sell their cigarettes on the black market. But it was unofficially agreed that they could use them to tip the German women who cleaned up the houses we lived in, and to purchase fresh vegetables for the mess, and even a haystack or two to feed our horses.

The summer was spent riding, sailing in the Baltic and visiting Denmark. Miles wrote: 'The Battalion next moved to Neumunster where our main task was to guard about 10,000 German civilian prisoners who were in a brick factory compound. They were being sifted by allied intelligence officers. I often wondered when one saw them in their shabby clothing as to how many were horrible Nazi activists and whether they would ever be discovered.' This was the time of Nuremberg, with the Control Commission processing senior Nazi suspects for trial.

At this time Miles had an extremely distressing and formative experience.

I was on a court martial of a Scots private who had murdered a German NAAFI storeman and we found him guilty. He was sentenced to be shot and our battalion was ordered to carry this out. I had to attend as a member of the court to identify the accused, he was totally repentant and came from a split home in the Gorbals of Glasgow and it was awful. At dawn the ten best shots marched into the miniature range, grounded arms, marched out and the Adjutant put live rounds in two of the rifles. They then marched back and fired at a white disc over the breast of the private, who was in no way dead, for it was known the bullets went straight through the body, so the Provost-Marshal was ready to shoot him in the head with his revolver. I have always condemned capital punishment after this and anyhow I think the Army gave up executions by shooting about this time.

In October 1946 they moved to Berlin where Miles as usual entertained his men by showing them round the Potsdam Palaces in the Russian Zone. Senior ranks used to go to the opera in East Berlin. 'I spoke Yorkshire German which I had learned at Ampleforth. I found it

very useful. Although fraternisation was still discouraged, both the officers and Guardsmen were beginning to meet Germans and I can
remember a small cocktail party in one of the officers' billets, but we
were still cold towards them.'

The Commanding Officer, John Davies, went back to England for
Christmas leaving me in command, as there was no Senior Major.
We were suddenly ordered to Wuppertal to take over some very
bombed-out barracks, which had earlier housed displaced persons
who had stolen everything, and still contained German prostitutes
in an attic. I nearly persuaded the GOC to let us postpone the
move until after Christmas but we had to go on 17 December. It
was a great tribute to the Battalion's morale and discipline that all
went so well. We had some very experienced company commanders and a magnificent Quartermaster, Johnny Pratt. The men
were wonderful with great inter-company rivalry. Christmas in a
battalion was great fun in those days.

The spring brought a new senior major and a new Commanding
Officer, Geordie Gordon-Lennox. Miles cunningly posted his company
away before their arrival.

In February 1947 I chose my company for a commitment to guard
the Commander-in-Chief at Ostenwalde. He was Sir Sholto
Douglas of the RAF. I discovered that Montgomery had been at
Ostenwalde when the war ended. His guard company had been
disbanded there. We found armoured cars in the stables, endless
mess and a disgraceful muddle which we put right. On our return
to Wuppertal I organised a swan to Prague of four officers –
myself, Hugo Money-Coutts, Reresby Sitwell and Donald Pearce
with four Guardsmen and two jeeps with trailers. This took a lot
of planning; we had to get petrol from the Americans as we passed
through Frankfurt. We went beyond Prague to the Tatra Moun-
tains and into Poland. We were rather cold-shouldered by the
Russians but Czechoslovakia was still friendly. We had sixteen
punctures due to the endless horse traffic which dropped nails for
our tyres to pick up.

Miles was then again in court in Duisburg trying Germans for shooting RAF pilots who had bailed out. 'They were clearly guilty, but the

stories told of the big RAF raids of the streets on fire made horrible hearing. The Germans were stealing potatoes out of the farmers' fields, but did not actually starve. We rode our horses, marched, drilled and trooped the colour watched by the Americans.'

One highlight of the Battalion's tour at Wuppertal was a battlefield tour of Waterloo. Virtually all of the officers and senior NCOs participated. Moreover the Battalion organised a glamorous Waterloo Ball. On other occasions the Battalion's armoured battles of 1945 were studied with interest. Some of the Guards' knocked out tanks were still there. The Earl of Kimberley enjoyed telling the story of how he 'had been left with Peter Carrington in Brussels to collect the remnants of the 2nd Armoured Battalion's tanks in 1944. We stayed in a very comfortable hotel which was full of every luxury and all for free. After a while, we realised that it was a very high class brothel!' Another officer, Major T. Tufnell, MC, recalled his amazement at the large amounts of sugar, food and champagne found in Brussels on its liberation whereas thousands were dying of malnutrition in Holland.

In 1947 General Julian Gascoigne, Military Attaché at the Embassy in Washington, asked for Miles to be his assistant. The Regimental Adjutant wrote to the 2nd Grenadiers' Adjutant as follows:

> The Military Secretary's Branch to agree to it, secondly, the Lieutenant-Colonel would like it suggested that he realises that Miles wants a job in England, but there is nothing suitable at the present time and, therefore, it is advisable that he accepts a good appointment of this kind though overseas.
>
> For your very private information his family also are of the same opinion as the Lieutenant-Colonel that, if acceptable, he is well advised to take it knowing how restless he is.

This was a wonderful opportunity, being one year after the Berlin airlift, at the height of the Cold War and the beginning of the Korean War. At the centre of the solutions to all these problems lay Anglo-American cooperation, particularly military.

2
Romance and Marriage

[It seemed appropriate, if not entirely chronological, to place this chapter between the two chapters by Tony Chambers on Miles's years as a soldier. G.N.]

In the summer of 1946, while on leave in England, Miles happened to run into an old friend of his, a fellow adjutant called Bobby Steele. The latter told Miles he had recently met, working on the watercress beds at her family home, a most charming 'Catholic blonde' girl. He thought Miles would like her and should get to know her. Thus, on a visit shortly afterwards to Alresford in Hampshire, Miles for the first time met Anne Constable Maxwell whose home was nearby. They hit it off extremely well but there was no time for anything like romance at this stage. It was to be more than two years, in fact, before Miles, in quite different circumstances, met Anne again. Meanwhile an important new development in his life had occurred, as already recorded by Tony Chambers.

Miles, still based in Berlin, received, in September 1947, news of a cable from General Julian Gascoigne, at that time head of the British Military Mission at the Pentagon in Washington DC, asking that Miles should join his staff. This cable not only came at a sensitive moment in Miles's career, but it was to have, if only indirectly, extremely important consequences. Now that the war was over, Miles had had to give thought to the future. The decision as to whether or not to stay in the Army depended on what opportunity presented itself next. Julian Gascoigne's cable clinched matters.

Miles by his own account was 'thrilled to stay on in the Army' and duly sailed on the *Queen Mary* for New York on 9 October. His job was to be Military Assistant, or 'GSO II', to Julian Gascoigne on the British Army Staff in Washington. Half the work would be in the Pentagon and half at the British Army Staff HQ at 1910 K. Street, NW, where Miles's office was to be located. Julian Gascoigne was an old friend, having commanded Miles's battalion in the early part of the war.

For the first part of his time in Washington, Miles stayed with the Gascoignes at their house at 34th Street. It so happened, however, that a cousin of Miles was living in Washington at the time, namely Margaret, the wife of Johnny Walker. Margaret was the sister of David (Lord) Perth, and a first cousin of Bernard Norfolk; their mother Angela (born Constable Maxwell) and Gwendolen Duchess of Norfolk were sisters. It was thus that Miles and Anne were both related to the Norfolks, though not directly to each other. Margaret Walker and Johnny were old friends and Miles lost no time in getting in touch with them. He became, for a short time, a guest in the Walker's beautiful house in Georgetown, while looking for permanent accommodation of his own.

Miles's stay with the Walkers lasted for five very happy months. It was an ideal and restful 'home from home' for him, apart from which the Walkers knew 'everyone' in Washington. Miles rapidly became popular and much in demand for parties. Washington is, and always was, a centre of intense social activity (often linked to political and business ambitions) and Miles's social credentials were not lost on the ambitious and snobbish local hostesses. The more percipient, however, were quick to discover that he was instantly put off by anything that smacked of pretentiousness or social climbing. His popularity however, then as always, was due quite as much to his instantly and infectiously friendly nature as to the fact of who he was.

After his sojourn with the Walkers, Miles moved into lodgings of his own at 28/29 O Street. He was, by then, thoroughly settled in his job which had been interesting from the beginning and had grown in importance after his arrival. This was largely – according to Sir Vivian Gabriel, who was head at the time of the British Purchasing Commission in Massachusetts Avenue – because of the enthusiasm and industry Miles put into the job. Expeditions away from the capital were part of the attractions.

A few weeks after his arrival he had joined General Julian and his wife Joyce Gascoigne on a trip by car to Fort Bliss, Oklahoma, as well as Fort Worth and El Paso in Texas on the Mexican border. The trip lasted from 8 to 23 December 1947 and Miles noted in his diary that 'to visit these centres was a great experience at that time'. North America, as he was to explain years later, opened new horizons for him, despite the width and variety of his previous travels (soon to become even more extensive) in different parts of the world.

His work, however, though interesting, was exacting and tiring and Miles earned and enjoyed his periods of leave at Christmas and the following Easter. The first was spent at the Palisades in New York State with Tony Lamont with whom he was friendly through Christopher Emmet, who had just married his sister Miranda. His second period of leave was spent in Bermuda with Eric and Lavender Russell, the former being a fellow Grenadier. Such periods of leave were refreshing but all too brief, his next being in England in July 1948, but only for one week. His official trips, however, were to him, with his restless energy and inquiring mind, in their own way as good as a holiday.

September brought some exciting and dramatic events. Miles got to know about a visit being made by Anne Constable Maxwell to the USA to stay with her American aunt, Isabel. She and her husband Bill Griffin had a Manhattan apartment in Park Avenue and also a farm at Peapack, New Jersey, which was within easy driving distance from New York City.

Miles was invited to stay with the Griffins for the last weekend in October, where he met Anne (properly) for the second time. Thereafter, things began happening with exciting, indeed bewildering speed, as shown by Anne's and Miles's letters written at the time (from which Anne has kindly let me quote).

Miles was immediately smitten by Anne's charms while she, though she took an instant liking to Miles, was slower to react in kind to his obvious attraction to her. This was characteristic of their respective natures, Miles being ever impetuous and impatient once he had made up his mind.

They corresponded and Miles was invited to spend Christmas at Peapack, soon after which Anne and 'Aunt Isa', as they called her in the family, sailed to Hawaii and stayed at Waikiki Beach in Honolulu for the sake of Aunt Isa's TB lung.

Aunt Isa suddenly received a wire from Miles asking if it would be convenient for him to come and stay at the same hotel for a week from 29 January, and, if so, would she kindly book him a room? The wire came on 21 January and Isabel immediately reserved accommodation for Miles, who duly arrived on the 29th (this was now 1949). Two days

later Anne wrote to her parents. It was a long letter and a very sensible
one for a girl of nineteen who was well aware of Miles's feeling but too
balanced to be swept off her feet. 'Now quite obviously', she wrote,
'one doesn't fly 1,200 miles for a six day stay, taking into consideration
the cost of the ticket which comes to roughly $500, unless one has quite
a definite purpose in view.' She went on to say 'In other words Miles is
very much in love with me and wants to marry me.'

They had similar tastes and interests and Miles liked the same sports
as she did, especially riding and hunting. The latter was enthusiastically
pursued in and around the part of the country lived in by the Griffins in
New Jersey, and Miles was to take part in several enjoyable hunts there
when staying during weekends later that same winter. The hunting was
the 'real thing,' involving the actual chasing of a fox. It was not mere
'drag'.

Anne, moreover, was quick to spot one of Miles's more unobtrusive
but very characteristic qualities, namely his inquiring mind and immediate thirst for the fullest possible knowledge of some subject or situation that was new to him. Anne was also aware, but in a distinctly
detached and objective fashion, of various material and worldly things
about Miles and his probable future. There was always the chance of
his eventually becoming Duke of Norfolk. To this her immediate reaction was 'Frankly, I cannot quite see myself in the role of a Duchess. I
should hate to have to open a bazaar!'

Then Anne says in her letter, getting to the main point of the news,
'You are probably wondering how the great romance is going. I am
really getting awfully fond of Miles although I am not in love with him
yet. Only time can tell about that, I guess.'

Perhaps the best way to summarise Anne's thoughts at this crossroads in her life is to be found further down in the letter already quoted.
It exhibits Anne's combination of worldly and spiritual wisdom. She
insisted that they still did not know each other well enough to make a
final decision possible; but she ended her very long letter on a hopeful
note based on what I have called that 'spiritual wisdom' produced by
her profound faith. Prompted by this she asks her parents to 'pray a lot
that this thing turns out the right way and that when I feel the time has
come I make the right decision. Aunt Isa is being wonderful. She is all
for it as she has grown extremely fond of Miles but she understands my
feelings perfectly.'

It is interesting to note not only how true these sentiments ring on their own, but also how they correspond to what Miles himself was thinking – as can be seen from what he wrote himself to various people a few days later. Despite Anne's hesitation, moreover – Miles being on the point of going back to Washington – all was quite suddenly quickly decided. Miles, a few days later, was to write in his diary: 'I returned on February 5, engaged!'

Anne lost no time in telling her parents the exciting news. She did so on 7 February in a succinct cable which merely read: 'We have progressed to a happy conclusion. Tell no one have written. So much love to all from Aunt Isa and me, Anne.' Her parents immediately cabled their delighted congratulations to which Anne wrote back to say 'Darling Mummy and Daddy, thank you so much for your cable. I am so glad that you are happy about it, although on that score I had no worries....'

It is noticeable how very much more relaxed and carefree this letter is compared to her previous one in which the stress of reaching a decision was inevitably apparent. By contrast, this letter rattles on with happy reporting of her activities and then plunging immediately into detailed plans for the future, including whom she would like to have as her bridesmaids. One of those she mentions as a choice for a bridesmaid was 'Adele' whom I was lucky enough to marry several years later. They had been close friends for some time and their friendship has lasted and blossomed through the years to be as close today as it ever was.

Anne was quick to share her happiness with her three younger sisters and brother in a bubbling-over letter of 18 February 1949.

Darling Diana, Carolyn, Rosemary and Peter,
    As Mummy may have told you, I have become engaged to a very nice man called Miles Fitzalan Howard ....

After explaining how they had got to know each other so quickly, Anne then wrote that after a few days of having 'so much fun together, swimming and walking and lying on the beach, we decided it would be a lovely idea if we spent the rest of our lives together'.

Anne was a changed person in every way, writing to tell everyone her wonderful news, and of course, making all sorts of plans for the future. Miles, meanwhile, back in Washington, was unprecedently happy. First and foremost, he wrote to Anne's parents, whom he had often met and actually knew quite well.

For all his puckish disdain of convention and his occasional irreverence, Miles was at all times, at heart, an old-fashioned English Catholic gentleman. The following letter to his parents-in-law to-be, as well as the subsequent one to Isabel Griffin, sheds light on his character and way of thinking.

Miles was a stickler for convention in affairs that really mattered and always concerned with good manners. This was one of the more important letters written by Miles, and I hope it will be thought appropriate that I have quoted almost all of it. It was sent from the British Joint Services Mission in Washington on 9 February 1949 – that is, two days after his return from Hawaii. The letter opens with some intentionally quaint phraseology:

7 February 1949

Dear Wing Comd. and Mrs. Maxwell,

May I marry your excellent daughter Anne? Having posed this tremendous question with due decorum I will continue in a lighter vein: (after all last time I saw Gerald he remarked my hat made me look like a bookie!)

I first met her about three years ago at Alresford and was madly intrigued but scared by the 12 years between 18 and 30.

Then, unexpectedly (after going to Washington), I was kindly invited by Isabel and Bill in Oct. I only saw her for a moment before the journey to N.Y. but the dart struck me. Henceforth I hunted madly. I was thrice frustrated before Xmas. Then I stayed and made up my mind. I wangled a return at the New Year which confirmed matters.

Anne gave me little encouragement, but I was determined to chase her and had to move to Honolulu. There, five days ago, we agreed to become secretly engaged and ask both our parents.

I am a staunch Catholic. Frankly I wish to lead the life of a Catholic layman, enter politics (later when more erudite at 40 or thereabouts) and generally carry on the traditions of my family. At the moment the Army is an excellent lair and anyhow it is little use and very boring to vegetate in England as a young man. We both love life and have the same ideas on children. I have always worked hard and lived on my wits; but I will inherit quite a pretty parcel which should satisfy even Anne's desires in dresses!

I love Anne; after Honolulu, when under the wise aegis of Isabel we really got to know each other, she loves me.

I am full of health and life and so is she. It is quite impossible to convey all that I wish to in a few tired sentences. (I arrived at 11 p.m. last night and have had a busy day in the office dealing with a mountain that had accrued.) But I must write tonight to beg your approval of our engagement.

We wish to keep it secret between the families for the moment.

Anne would like us to get married in July; so would I; but duties here look like dictating May or Dec. I will explore this.

I must to bed.

Yours very sincerely,

MILES

Two days later, Miles wrote to Isabel Griffin.

[*Note at head*] P.S. This is my best bread and butter letter to-date. Miles.

10 February 1949

Dear Aunt Isa,

(Henceforth, if you allow it, I will always so call you.) I cannot describe my feelings of gratefulness. It was almost entirely because of your wisdom that dear Anne has agreed to marry me. I am indeed now at the happiest moment of my life and know that even better days lie ahead. Thank you so very much. I have just received Anne's letter (I've had to send it to the cipher office!). In it she confirms all she said at Honolulu. It is all too wonderful and quite unmerited by me. Thank her for it deeply; I'll write very soon again to her.

I would like to set down in writing now to you, that I can promise you before God that I will always look after your niece and that you will never have reason to regret having brought us two together. We wooed together under God's eyes, and our very engagement has brought us both nearer to Him. I am in love now utterly and madly, and after Honolulu, Deo Gratias so is she. We both have the same background and as far as we can see the same 'future' ground, at any rate in our desires and principles.

I think Anne would not mind my telling you that we dug down into each other's depths. Our foundations are the most secure possible. We certainly covered a lot of ground in little more than a wink of an eye.

I have re-read the above so far; it sounds heavy and hackneyed; but realise every word is true.

Doubtless, darling Anne will read this (possibly before you, if I know her form!), in which case all my deepest love to her. Pray for us. Much love.

MILES

Here then was Miles with his feet firmly on the ground. It must not be forgotten, moreover, how quickly events had been moving. To make all the necessary arrangements, initially from abroad, and when Miles could not yet be sure of when he could get away on leave, naturally made life difficult. But being abroad, in the USA, had certain advantages for Anne. She went to a New York dressmaker, the same one who had made the gown for her coming-out dance two years before, to have her wedding dress made. The result was a wonderful creation that would not have been possible in an England stifled by clothes rationing. When the time came, the dress, not surprisingly, caused a sensation. Its train was a spectacular feature, several yards long.

While the grown-up bridesmaids (there were ten of them) had to find their own coupons for their dresses, the child bridesmaids, numbering six, had been thoughtfully catered for by Anne. While getting her wedding dress in New York, she had also bought the necessary amount of material for the child bridesmaids.

There was, in addition, another child attendant, her five-year-old brother Peter. He made a handsome page in his Fraser tartan kilt and white silk shirt. Peter grew up to have an extremely interesting career, travelling widely and working for several worthwhile and, in some cases, dangerous causes. In earlier days he had found his surname unexpectedly useful as, on one occasion he was stopped for speeding. When the policeman asked him who he was he replied 'I'm Constable Maxwell.' To this the officer apologetically said, 'Oh sorry, Constable, didn't recognise you in plain clothes.'

Miles and Anne met as often as possible in the next few weeks, mostly for weekends at the farm in Peapack. Anne came once or twice to Washington and asked Johnny and Margaret Walker, with whom she stayed, whether their daughter Gillian (a cousin from a different side of both Miles and Anne) would like to be a bridesmaid. Margaret was delighted and plans were duly made.

Miles and Anne met occasionally in New York where they busily shopped between bouts of sightseeing and visiting the theatre. Much of the arranging of the wedding had to be done by letter and telegram. It was a miracle of cooperative arrangements that enabled the occasion to take place without a hitch on 4 July. Miles flew over at the end of June from the USA, as he only had a week's leave. Amazingly, everything turned out brilliantly well.

It was, in fact, hailed as the 'wedding of the year' by a press still starved of glamorous copy by the continuing austerity of postwar Britain. The social and fashion-conscious writers had a field-day with plenty of material to work on. One of the headlines was 'Watercress Girl Says Yes'.

The (London) *Evening Standard* for 4 July 1949 reported:

Miss Anne Maxwell, daughter of Wing-Commander and Mrs. Gerald C. Maxwell, was married at Brompton Oratory today in a wedding-gown – with-a-secret.

She brought it with her from America and its several yards long train got rolled into a ball on the steps of the Church. The bride-groom was Major Miles Fitzalan Howard, heir of Lord Howard of Glossop.

When they knelt at the chancel steps an attendant again had to disentangle the train. It was beyond the control of the bride's five year old brother Peter, who was her page.

The story went on to report that one of the grown-up bridesmaids was Miss Jean Kennedy, youngest sister of the future President John F. Kennedy, who had flown over from the USA. Sisters, cousins and friends helped to make up the other ten grown-up bridesmaids; one of the child bridesmaids was Lady Anne Fitzalan Howard, eleven-year-old daughter of the Duke and Duchess of Norfolk.

The twelve Grenadier Guardsmen who formed the guard of honour were in full-dress uniforms – tightly-fitting scarlet gold-braided tunics and bearskins.

The fashion-conscious *Harper's Bazaar* commented that 'the bride looked quite charming in her dress of white tulle, the bodice heavily embroidered in seed-pearls as was the headband which held her voluminous tulle veil in place'.

The same report went on to say that the bridesmaids 'made a pretty picture in white with bouquets of flame-coloured gladioli and roses, sprays of which were also fixed at the side of their skirts. The page, the bride's five year old brother Peter, looked very fine in his Fraser tartan kilt.'

The wedding service at the Oratory was conducted by Cardinal Griffin, Archbishop of Westminster, assisted by Miles's old friend Father James Forbes, OSB. The address was given by Monsignor Ronald Knox, another old friend. Ronnie – as so many people called him – was a very special character whom I got to know quite well some years after this. He was much in demand as a giver of addresses at weddings, funerals and similar occasions and was extremely good at it. This was true in spite of – or perhaps because of – the fact that his style was highly original. He was not a naturally effective orator, and could never speak in public extemporaneously. Every word was written out and his addresses were read. The subject matter, however, was so excellent that the result was invariably successful. He not only prepared his talks with great care, but he read them particularly well. He had a natural, and therefore palpably unaffected, gift for dramatic presentation.

On this particular occasion I remember his saying that marriage was often put forward as a suitable field for practising 'give and take'. His own recommendation was that what was called for was 'give and give'. It was certainly a precept which Miles and Anne followed.

Miles's brother Michael was best man and the reception was held at Claridge's where Bernard Norfolk made an apposite speech.

The bride and groom flew off early the next morning to Shannon Airport to spend a brief honeymoon of four days at the Dunraven Arms in Adare, County Limerick, one of the prettiest villages in Ireland. Then, Miles's short leave having come to an end, they were back in Washington by 10 July.

Later they had what Miles in his diary described as a 'proper honeymoon' generously provided by Bill Griffin. This was at an idyllic spot called Dewy Riddle Ranch at Sunlight Valley near Cody in Wyoming.

Back in Washington, after a short stay with the Walkers, they rented a little house called The Foxhole at 1673 34th Street.

Miles's stint with Julian Gascoigne was due to end in December. On the 10th of that month they sailed back to England on the *Queen Elizabeth*. They spent Christmas at Carlton, which Miles loved as much as ever.

For almost twenty years marriage was combined with further soldiering. From Anne's point of view it involved all the considerable challenges of being a mother and housekeeper as the wife of a regular Army officer. They kept on their house in Smith Street until 1952 when with the proceeds of its sale in 1956 they bought the delightful house called Bacres in the Hambleden Valley – near Henley-on-Thames. This was to be their principal home for the rest of their fifty-three years of married life; where, after Marsha's divorce, the gardener's cottage and garages were made into a charming house for her and her three children.

Their five children were born during these years: Tessa, born on 30 September 1950, married to Roderick (now the Earl of Balfour); Carina, born on 20 February 1952, and married to Sir David Frost; Marsha, born on 10 March 1953, who married Patrick Ryecart (divorced May 1995); Edward, now Duke of Norfolk, born on 2 December 1956 and married to Georgie Gore; and Gerald born on 13 June 1962 and married to Emma Roberts. When Tessa was one week old, Nanny Browning joined the family and brought up all the children, who loved her very much. Nanny Browning afterwards travelled with them all over the world. Like Miles himself, they have all grown up as members of an exceptionally united and happy family, as well as all being, in different ways, endowed with the Fitzalan Howard charm.

3

1950–1967

TONY CHAMBERS

In January 1950 Miles took over No. 1 Company, 3rd Grenadiers in Chelsea. In December Miles and Anne nearly killed themselves overturning on the ice outside Arras after staying in Rome with Nicky and Andrew Maxwell, Anne's aunt and uncle, who cannot have been best pleased as it was their car.

Miles's report on his return from Washington describes him as

> a very efficient officer, intelligent and conscientious. He has carried out all his duties exceptionally well and is very experienced in the ways and organisation of the Army.
>
> He has been away on the staff for a considerable period of his service which appears to make it a little difficult for him on occasions when dealing with junior officers who have only regimental experience. There is no reason for this difficulty but it will help him if he can remain regimentally employed at least through the next Battalion training period.
>
> There is no danger that any grass will ever grow under Major Fitzalan Howard's feet. He is a very able officer with a clear and quick brain and possesses the ability to pick out immediately the important points of any problem. His military knowledge is well above the average of his rank. He is a very experienced staff officer, and although the majority of recent years have been spent on the staff, I see no reason why he should not command a battalion very well. He has been of great value as senior major of the battalion and his loyalty, initiative together with his efficiency and determination to get things done have been an excellent example to all.

In July 1951 he flew to Libya to become senior major of the 1st Battalion. At that time it was under orders to fly to Persia to deal with

Moussadeq who had nationalised the Anglo-Iranian Oil Company (BP). This never took place and the Battalion returned to Windsor.

In February 1952 the King died and Miles, commanding at St James's Palace, saw Bernard and the Heralds proclaim Queen Elizabeth II. He looked after the Windsor end of the funeral with the King's Company furnishing the bearer party, led by CSM Clutton, who had won the MM attacking the SS near Belsen concentration camp.

A week later Carina was born in a London nursing home and joined the rest of the family in Smith Street to come under the care of Nanny Browning.

Miles was then appointed as a General Staff Officer Grade 1 to the Inter-Allied Tactical Study Group in Bonn commanded by General Beaufre. The idea was a think-tank to see how nuclear weapons could be best used tactically. Up until then nuclear armaments had only been thought of as having strategic applications. This was right up Miles's street, swanning around Europe viewing all the exercises with an inter-national group of military thinkers and living in comparative luxury at the Villa Albrecht above Bad Godesberg on the Rhine, where Marsha was born in March 1953.

Miles was on duty at the Coronation of Queen Elizabeth II as a Gold Staff Officer.

He left the study group in October 1954. His report reads:

French (Good) German (Fair). The French General Officer under whom he works has expressed to me his complete satisfaction, in fact his admiration for his work. He regards him as outstanding in the team he controls. When I have met him, Lt. Col. Fitzalan Howard has given me an excellent impression of efficiency, alert-ness and intelligence. He has the personality of a leader, and at the same time the ability to work harmoniously with others.

Field Marshal Montgomery endorsed this report, writing: 'I have known him very well for many years. He is a first-class officer in every way and is fit for promotion to substantive Lieutenant-Colonel and to command a battalion. I agree with this report throughout.'

In January 1955 Anne and Miles drove in their Humber Hawk to Port Said via Yugoslavia, Greece, Istanbul, Syria and Beirut, where they shipped to Alexandria because Israel/Palestine was out of bounds. This was a real adventure during the Cold War and before motorways. In

fact they had to put the car on a train between Salonica and Adrianople
because there was no road!

Miles then took over command of the 2nd Grenadiers in Golf
Course Camp at Port Said. The Middle East was then in its typical state
of turmoil with the Arab-Israeli dispute, the Russian infiltration into
Egypt, the jealousy and ambitions of the new Arab states. Britain was at
the centre of these troubles with its treaty commitments to Jordan and
the Baghdad Pact, whereby Britain guaranteed the Armistice line in
Palestine and the neutrality of the Canal Zone then owned by Britain
and France. The UK also needed to defend its oil interests in the Persian
Gulf.

Although the camp was dreary, the urban environment was a change
and officers' families lived in comfort in Port Fuad. Suez even boasted
the odd night club. The Commanding Officer took the Quartermaster,
Captain G. C. Hackett, to see a belly dancer on the dubious grounds
that they should know what the young officers were getting up to. The
English civil community in Port Said were not particularly friendly and
some chose not to fraternise with the Army in order to demonstrate
their non-involvement in the political situation. So some Grenadier officers joined the French Club where the food was excellent.

Miles's swanning skills came into full force with his responsibilities
for trials on the new FN rifle allowing him to send his troops to fight
the Mau Mau in Kenya, train the Iraqis in Kurdistan, and the Sudanese
in Khartoum. The training team was also sent to Tripoli. Needless to
say Miles had the greatest possible fun visiting all these efforts, staying
with the Leicesters in Khartoum and the Rifle Brigade in Nanyuki, the
centre of the Mau Mau campaign.

> We visited Alexandria and went up the Nile to Luxor and the
> Aswan Dam when Diana Constable Maxwell stayed with us. We
> visited Cyprus twice and finally I seized the opportunity to send a
> company to Aqaba, which meant we could swan into Jordan and
> Jerusalem. The officers, including their families, never stopped
> recounting what a wonderful year it was.

Miles commanded the Queen's Birthday Parade in the Canal Zone
in 1955 when there were more guardsmen on parade in Moascar than
on Horse Guards. He also ignored the order by the Foreign Office that
Cairo was out of bounds by getting the very friendly Egyptian officers

to invite and show his companies around the tourist sites. He said 'It would have been bad manners not to have accepted the invitation.' There was also a lot of sea work using barges to move ammunition. Bernard Gordon-Lennox recalls: 'We were not allowed to tie the barges up for safety reasons, but I did so by the quay near the French Canal Zone's offices. The Commanding Officer (Miles) got a bill for £2m and was most upset.'

It was time for the British to leave Egypt and Miles persuaded the authorities that his battalion would be the last to leave, on the dubious grounds that the Coldstream and Scots Guards had played a lesser part in the 1882 battle of Tel-el-Kebir.

All our camp was perfectly clean when we left in secrecy during the night of 2nd April 1956 but, as so often happens, the Officers' Mess was in bad order. Peter Thwaites and I cleaned it up… I travelled back with the battalion to Windsor and Anne drove home with Diana and Michael Bayley. We bought Bacres for £6,200. Eddie was born on the 2nd December and Dickie Birch Reynardson ordered all the champagne in Barracks for a joint sergeants' and officers' party, for which I had to pay!

In March 1957 Miles commanded the parade in Paris for the Queen's visit. The parade consisted of the Brigade of Guards, a Naval gun team and a RAF drill team, all accompanied by the Grenadier band and the pipes of the Argylls.

Miles was then appointed Commander of the British Military Mission (Brixmis) at Potsdam in East Germany. As an introduction to this job I quote from Miles's foreword to Tony Geraghty's history of Brixmis.

Most of the secret history of the Cold War, so far, has been more exposed by representatives of the former Soviet empire than by those of us who played from the other end of the pitch. The memoirs of Sudoplatov (*A Soviet Spymaster*), Oleg Kalugin and Gordievsky as well as Kim Philby and John Cairncross pile up like bricks in a new historical wall. The only other British voice to be heard, from within the secret world, has been that of the MI5 veteran Peter Wright in *Spy Catcher*. That is also a story of failure or suspected failure on the British side, a tale of penetration or suspected penetration by the KGB, a tale of suspicion and betrayal.

The reality was different and vitally included Brixmis, the military liaison Mission behind the Iron Curtain, which I had the honour to command for two years as an unexpected change from orthodox, regimental soldering. The Cold War ended with a bloodless victory and the victory was ours. We got close enough to the Russians to respect them as people, as well as to photograph their military secrets. Under the original agreement the Americans, Russians, British and French were allowed to inspect each other's military exercises to reduce Cold War tension.

As Miles pointed out, the real importance of this was not to look at each other's latest weaponry or even numbers, but to check for logistical build-ups necessary for any attack. For 'D' Day each soldier required 80 tonnes. By 1957 this had gone up to 200 tonnes. Miles was always convinced that they were never going to attack because he could detect no such build-up.

Miles took over at a very sensitive time. His predecessor Brigadier Wynn-Pope had had to retire from the Army prematurely after a serious run-in with the East German Secret Police (Stasi) who were increasingly taking over from the Russians in East Germany. The Russians removed Wynn-Pope's pass and both the Brits and the Russians looked for a safe pair of hands who would calm things down, hence Miles's appointment.

Tony Geraghty wrote:

Miles was a soldier's soldier. As a subaltern he had commanded the regiment's anti-tank platoon during a hard-fought rearguard action against the Wehrmacht at Dunkirk in 1940. By the time the war had turned, he was a brigade major of the 4th Armoured Brigade in the bitterly-fought Italian campaign all the way from Sicily to the Sangro. Equally useful, from Whitehall's point of view, he was untainted by any intelligence background. He had no 'form' so far as the KGB was concerned. At short notice, he was posted to Brixmis.

Miles commented: 'It transpired that I had been chosen because Pat Robertson, a former Grenadier who was working in MI5, had recommended me as having no intelligence background, yet having a crude knowledge of French and not being too stupid.'

Brixmis was much more important to British Intelligence than Soxmis to Russian intelligence, which had open access to military periodicals, technical journals etc. The Russians were very keen to maintain this advantage by frustrating Brixmis efforts illegally. Miles was arrested ten times and kept for up to forty-eight hours before release. The Russian advantage was compounded because Kim Philby handed over to them all Brixmis plans. This James Bond existence combined with a very attractive Berlin social life, operas, riding in the Grunewald and a lovely house overlooking the lake.

Miles typically broke the ice with a joke, on meeting his Soviet equivalent running Soxmis. 'I said to General Epenchin "I am very sad to see a young officer like you so bald", to which he replied through his interpreter "Just tell the Brigadier I am bald at the front because I work so hard; he is bald at the back which means too many women." From then on I could make jokes, even rude jokes with the Russians, and it didn't matter. The Russians were real soldiers, infantry soldiers full of jokes themselves.'

Thereafter the American, French and British had to side-track the East German police, called the Narks or more properly Stasi. The problem was a member of the MI6 team in Berlin, one George Blake, who had access to all their plans. Miles noted that whatever his team targeted was well covered by the Stasi Narks. He tried decoys, false trails, practically anything but 'they always knew where we were going. We should have spotted this, but we didn't. George Blake who gave all our tour programmes to the East Germans was arrested for spying in April 1961.'

Miles's command ran from 1957 (the year in which the Russians demonstrated their technical missile superiority by putting the first astronaut into space) to 1959, the year of the second Berlin crisis. The mission was infested by eavesdropping devices so that 'we went into the gardens to whisper, and even then, the flower beds were probably bugged'. Despite the Khrushchev effect, CND protesters and communist witch-hunting leading up to the 1962 Cuban missile crisis, Miles was convinced that the Third World War would not happen.

I never believed there would be a real invasion. We saw the Red Army manoeuvres but if it was the real thing one would see the vast echelons of ammunition and supplies of fuel moving forward. They were not there. I never thought there was going to be a war; and that was the tenor of my reports to my headquarters. At parties back home, when we heard people talking about the Russian threat, we said it was rubbish, they had no intention of attacking.

Not even Miles's *sang-froid* could prevent the near-destruction of mission buildings in his second year of command. Following the US invasion of Lebanon and the British support for Jordan, there was a Soviet backlash and Miles recalls 'There's a bit of a riot going on in Potsdam.' The mob attacked the Brixmis mission chanting 'Hands off Middle East'.

Considerable damage was done. Miles said to the Soviet Town Commandant of Potsdam, Sergeyv, 'You promised me personally that there would be no violence against the mission. It was a solemn promise from a soldier to a soldier and you broke it.' The Soviet colonel was crying and that night at a party at the Officers' Club in Berlin Miles handed out portions of the scorched Union flag. It was the end of the original mission site and Brixmis moved to new premises found and decorated by Anne.

Almost exactly a year later Sergeyv asked Miles to come down to the Soviet Liaison Office at Potsdam, where he produced a pile of crisp new English fivers, and slowly counted out £1,200 owing in damages. He did not even ask for a receipt. Despite all this aggression, Miles, the safe pair of hands, had his hands tied, almost amounting to appeasement. He noted that the lack of coordination amongst the three Western teams often meant that a Stasi hunt stirred up by one ally would compromise another. Miles's initiative meant integrated tours more clearly defined and specially allocated week by week and all tours were debriefed at the US mission office before returning home. It took another year to integrate the individualistic French into the system but Miles talked them round. When Miles left, he handed over to Brigadier John Packard, who lasted just a year in the job and then, like Wynn-Pope, left the Army completely. It is to Miles's absolute credit that he confronted the illegal East German takeover from the Russians with his career intact. This may have been due to his wonderful sense of humour, particularly appreciated by the Russians. He once said 'These Russians have as good a sense of humour as Irish Guards sergeants.'

At the end of his Brixmis tour, Miles and Anne left Berlin with some regret, but well-equipped with splendid East German china. Miles was awarded a CBE.

1960 was spent at the Imperial Defence College, the school for potential generals. This involved a tour of not only the industrial north but also the Indian and Arabian continents. Miles lectured the Staff College on the Russian Army and Brixmis, which had them all laughing and was an outstanding success.

Miles was then appointed as Brigade Commander of 70th King's African Rifle Brigade in 1961, just three months after Kenyatta's release from prison, and two years after Macmillan's 'winds of change' speech.

When I took over in September 1961, there were 150 white officers and no black officers, but when I left the command after two and a half years I had made over one hundred black officers. I pointed out to Profumo, the Minister for War, that although my black officers were clearly not as intelligent as the whites, they were better than the black officers being trained by the Russians and we obviously helped to save Kenya, but it must be admitted that things went much awry in Uganda with the promotion of Idi Amin.

Miles learned Swahili at London University and practised it on his friends for many years afterwards. He climbed Kilimanjaro, met Kenyatta and an endless stream of British military and political dignitaries in the run up to Kenyan elections and independence. His family lived in a wonderful house surrounded by gardens and stables, near Nanyuki, overlooking Mount Kenya. Here his younger son Gerald was born on 13 June 1962.

With the appointment of Malcolm MacDonald, the son of Ramsay MacDonald, as Governor, Kenya had to be prepared for independence. Miles seems to have been the first person to realise that therefore the Kenyan Army had to be officered by Kenyan officers. When he took over there were no black officers, although there had been in the First World War. Very possibly Miles's greatest contribution to history was his determination to train and commission native officers, against the views of a Colonial establishment which had only recently experienced the Mau Mau terror. He was not popular for this policy but his personality won over everyone. It was not his fault that the ludicrously short time-frame meant that he had to do this in a hurry, and that the Kikuyu tribe who were the new politicians were not recruited into the KAR, because of their Mau Mau involvement. In the event it worked and gave Kenya a great measure of stability, even surviving the so-called 1964 mutinies, throughout Jomo Kenyatta's presidency. It was only later under Daniel Arap Moi that things started to go wrong. All this political expediency has to be seen against the Shifta terrorist invasion from Somaliland. These kinds of bush fire 'wars' are seen by the untutored observer as being faintly *Boy's Own* or Kipling. In fact, the Shifta terrorists were ruthless and the stories of what they did to their prisoners have no place in this family reading.

In August 1963 Miles led 70 Brigade in a demonstration of strength to impress the Shiftas. As a recently commissioned 2nd Lieutenant in the Oxford Officer Training Corps, I took part attached to 11th Battalion, King's African Rifles. This was one of the highlights of my life: the whole Brigade was on its feet, man-packing everything including the gunners packing the 105 Howitzers. We had two animal transport companies of mules sure-footed and wonderful and apart from their loads everything was air-dropped. There were no vehicles. Miles as Brigadier walked with his Brigade Headquarters behind the lead battalion along the jebel tops. It was only at night that we went down to collect the water. There were of course helicopters which provided the only casualty, a Samburu tribesman, who fell on his spear when one landed in his village. Our RAMC doctor stitched him up, surrounded by his admiring villagers.

Miles's Brigade Headquarters contained remarkable characters apart from himself. The brigade major was 'Mad Mitch' (Lieutenant Colonel Colin Mitchell), his administrative staff officer was David Ramsbottom, later Adjutant-General and Inspector of Prisons, and the intelligence officer was Bill Coppen-Gardiner, who had distinguished himself with an MC in the Mau Mau campaign.

Colin Mitchell, who led his Argylls into the Crater in Aden four years later, wrote in his autobiography:

Relaxing one evening after a long safari by Land Rover, I can remember sitting with an evening drink in the small KAR post at Wajir. Miles Fitzalan Howard, Pat Ross and Torquil Matheson were all laughing away about some incident during the day; the sun was sinking and with the cool evening breeze blowing across the desert, it was idyllic. I can remember thinking: 'This is the best soldiering I shall ever know. Nothing could be better than this.' I think perhaps the others might have felt the same at heart because now, six years later, we have all prematurely retired – but what memories we have of those days together in the old Colonial Empire. I would not have missed it for a king's ransom.

In these final years of British rule I was extremely fortunate in being a Brigade Major to Brigadier Miles Fitzalan Howard. He was a man of astonishing vitality and enthusiasm whose leadership and drive forced through a crash programme for the commissioning of African officers which undoubtedly saved the new Kenya Army when Jomo Kenyatta took over the reins of Government. Future historians, reviewing the contribution of the British race to the advancement of mankind, may be struck by the important part which seconded British officers played in the encouragement of the emergent peoples. Miles Howard deserves a footnote to himself as he gave us all a great sense of purpose.

Miles Howard was a great traveller, a 'swanner' as the army term puts it. We travelled the length and breadth of East Africa together from Lake Rudolf to Dar-es-Salaam and from Uganda to Lamu Island – an old Arab slave port in the Indian Ocean. These safaris were quite magnificent and with our responsibility for Internal Security Operations throughout the land were a combination of business with pleasure.

Miles was then promoted major general to command the First Division in Germany. Given that there were then only four fully manned and equipped divisions and that their commanders rotated every three years, his achievement in getting this appointment should not be underestimated.

For the following I am indebted to James Tedder, an old friend, who was Miles's ADC.

Respected by all ranks, he seemed to create an atmosphere of fun despite deep down being a highly professional soldier. The Sergeants' Mess had a great affection for him. Frequently he would poke their tummies with his cane if they were on the large side or take off their berets if he thought their hair was receding.

Obviously there was a comparison with his own! He made every-one relax and feel comfortable in his presence.

He was very generous. He once gave me a cheque for the back wheels of my car and for a new suitcase as I was frequently late on parade and my suitcases left a lot to be desired. A hidden message I think! He had very high standards, and a lovely sense of humour.

He never wanted preferential treatment, always quietly remaining at the back of the room despite his elevated position.

Once he overheard someone talking about him when he arrived at a party saying 'Who is that man in the scruffy raincoat?' He always laughed about this story, but never bore a grudge.

Whilst travelling to do my first GOC's Inspection he said: 'Today is going to be a happy day.' I asked why in particular and he said 'Because they have been working up for this inspection for months and I know they will be immaculate. However please just look in the back of a 3-tonner. Take any one you like and see if it's clean. I bet it will be. That's all that needs to be done, apart from enjoying yourself.'

Enjoying life was the key, as witnessed by his inspection of the Black Watch. All guardsmen know that the Black Watch is the nearest thing to perfection outside the Brigade of Guards. Miles turned to his ADC and said 'We will turn out the guard when we arrive.' The guard duly turned out in kilts and white gaiters, the General inspected them and then turning to the sergeant of the guard asked 'Does your fire hose work?', to which the reply came 'Corporal.' At which the corporal of the guard turned on the hose, there was a delay and then the hydrant exploded up the corporal's kilt. The General made sure that he visited the Corporals' Mess after lunch to make amends. He was a soldier's soldier and they loved him.

His final posting was Director of Military Service Intelligence. He fell out with his boss for quite simple reasons. The Army and indeed the other two services exaggerated the probability of a Soviet nuclear attack, preceded by a Soviet conventional attack, in order to stop cuts in the Armed Forces. Miles, because he was intelligent and with his Brixmis experience convincing him that the Russians were not going to attack because of the lack of ordnance build-up, told his Chiefs that there was no threat.

His boss and the Army Chief disliked this plain speaking because it allowed the then Labour Government to make further Army cuts. He fell out with his boss, left the Army and joined Fleming's. 'Air Marshal McGuire told me I was not recommended to succeed him as Director of Military Intelligence which greatly depressed me. He and Air Chief Marshal Earle decided I knew too little about Whitehall. I was outraged, for he knew almost nothing about intelligence, and it was to my mind a scandal. Dick Goodwin, the Military Secretary, took up my case, as did the CIGS, General Sir James Cassels, but I had by that time decided to leave.'

PART THREE
Standard Bearer

I

The Norfolks

When Miles left the Army in September 1967 he knew that sooner or later, given normal expectation of life, he would be Duke of Norfolk. It was not something that – had it been left to him – he would ever have wished. It would bring with it, too, a challenging burden of inherited service and responsibility.

Duke Bernard was merely a cousin – Miles was descended from the second son of the 13th Duke of Norfolk. This chapter takes a brief look at the history of an illustrious family.

The Howard Dukes of Norfolk went back nearly 500 years, with the creation, as 1st Duke, of Sir John Howard for his services to King Richard III, who has acquired such a sinister reputation, deservedly or not, at the hands of most historians. John Howard's complicity in the cruel fate of Richard's nephew, Edward IV, one of the 'Princes of the Tower', remains uncertain. He was slain fighting for King Richard on the Field of Bosworth, the battle that was to inaugurate the Tudor age. Happier by far are the memories bequeathed by Thomas, 2nd Duke of Norfolk, who, by the time of his death in 1524, had risen to such eminence that his funeral assumed unprecedentedly magnificent proportions. Allowing for the fact that England had not yet broken with Rome, the 2nd Duke was honoured on his death by what was little less than a liturgical extravaganza, even by medieval Catholic standards. The solemn prolonged obsequies were worthy of a man deserving, in a very different religious-social atmosphere, to be described as a standard-bearer for Catholic and many other causes.

Not only was the funeral of the 2nd Duke unprecedented in its opulence, but nothing like it has even been seen since. The antiquary John Weever recorded, drawing on records then available but now destroyed, that 'no nobleman was ever to be buried in such style again'. An apparently small but not insignificant fact is that his will signed on 31 May 1524 was the last in which a subject signed himself as 'we'.

The 2nd Duke's claim to have preponderant influence in public affairs (in an England still Catholic) would have been incontestable had it not been for the appearance on the public stage of Thomas Wolsey. Whereas the latter was a highly successful upstart, Thomas Earl of Surrey, as he originally was, had in 1513 ended for ever the Scottish military threat against England at the decisive Battle of Flodden, and been rewarded with the restoration of the Dukedom of Norfolk in 1514. This came about by way of the removal of the action taken against his father, the first Howard Duke of Norfolk who had posthumously lost his title by attainder.[1] This was because he had supported, to the point of death, the Yorkist King Richard III, the adversary of Henry Tudor, now King of England (as Henry VII) by way of a claim through the Lancastrian line. To quote the words of his epitaph, the former Earl of Surrey was 'honourably restored to his right name of Duke of Norfolk' in a magnificent ceremony at Lambeth Palace on Candlemas Day, 1514.

For his role in the Battle of Flodden the 2nd Duke (then still Earl of Surrey) came to be remembered as 'The Flodden Duke'. He outwitted and outfought the Scottish army, despite being outnumbered by two to one, after James IV of Scotland invaded England and declared war on Henry VIII in 1513. England was saved from being menaced by Scotland and the two kingdoms were united less than a century later. Flodden, moreover, was the most glorious military triumph in Howard family history. Miles, in his characteristically bantering but always good-hearted fashion, never failed to tease Scottish visitors to Arundel about the battle.

In his capacity as Earl Marshal, moreover, Norfolk showed that his Catholic sympathies were no bar to his vigorous suppression of the 'May Day' riots of 1513, chiefly organised by a Catholic priest called Father Beale. They presented an ugly example of a certain xenophobia from which England has never been able fully to free itself, in that the riots were directed against such hated foreigners – mostly French or Flemish – as immigrant artificers and merchants in the City of London.

Only a few years after that duke's death things began to change so radically in England – particularly with regard to religion – that an

---

1 There is a difference of opinion among heraldic experts, some of whom maintain that because of the attainder against the supposedly 1st Duke of Norfolk, the man usually referred to as '2nd Duke' was in reality the first to hold the title. By this reckoning, Miles was the 16th not the 17th Duke of Norfolk.

entirely new era in the history of the Norfolk family was set in train. As John Martin Robinson put it in his excellent history of the family,[2] 'Within twenty years the whole ethos of which his [the 2nd Duke's] funeral was a last, but by no means undistinguished, witness would have been undermined.' Such obsequies Robinson adds 'marked the end of the Middle Ages in England'. It was not, however, the death of Catholic England.[3]

It was at this point that there arrived on the scene Thomas, 3rd Duke of Norfolk, described by Miles as 'that old rogue'.

The description was one of masterly understatement. The 3rd Duke, despite a surface charm, was unscrupulous and ruthless. The fact that he slowed down, without actually arresting, the moves toward Reformation – and the ultimate eradication of Romanism – was due more to his ultra-conservatism than any personal devoutness as a Catholic. For political reasons, however, he fell foul of the Crown and in 1547 was attainted and condemned to death. He was saved by the fact that King Henry VIII died first – on the very day that Norfolk was to have been beheaded. He was reprieved to spend the whole of the next reign, that of Edward VI, imprisoned in the Tower of London.

Edward VI, son of Jane Seymour, had been raised as a Protestant but remained a minor for the whole of his short reign (1547-1553). Power was wielded by the Protector Somerset, who had secured this critical position after a bitter struggle with the same (3rd) Duke of Norfolk. Under Somerset's Protectorship England was steered irrevocably in a Protestant direction. This raises a fascinating question. Had Norfolk, and not Somerset, secured the Protectorship for these critical years, would history have been different? Would his innate conservatism, rather than any Catholic idealism, have preserved the basically Catholic status quo until the accession of the Catholic Mary Tudor in 1553? We shall never know.

Remarkably, the duke survived to be restored to his former offices and powers by the succession of Queen Mary, at whose coronation he presided as Earl Marshal.

2 Dr John Martin Robinson, *The Dukes of Norfolk*, OUP, 1982.
3 The abundance of detail about Thomas, 2nd Duke of Norfolk is due to the unusually long autobiographical inscriptions originally adorning his monument in Thetford Priory. It was on this, as then still available as a source, that Weever relied in his *Ancient Funeral Monuments Within the United Monarchies of Great Britain, Ireland and the Islands Adjacent*, 1631.

Religious vicissitudes have thus played a major part in Norfolk family history. No example of this is more curious than that of the next holder of the title, Thomas 4th Duke of Norfolk, who held this position from 1554 until 1572. He was implicated in the so-called Ridolfi plot whose object was to replace Queen Elizabeth with the Catholic Mary Stuart. The duke was not a Catholic, and his supposed implication in the plot was a clever fabrication by Elizabeth's most able and unscrupulous super-spy servants Burghley and Walsingham.

What was true, however, was that the duke did want to marry the self-same Mary Stuart and to see her restored to her rightful throne of Scotland. After an extremely complicated sequence of events, the charges against the 4th Duke were finally made to stick and he was executed and attainted. Robinson calls him 'the tragic hero of the Howard family' whose 'death in 1572 marks the end of an epoch in the aesthetic and religious as well as the political history of England'. The attainder against him, moreover, had a devastating effect on the family. It lasted for nearly a century during which the dukedom went into abeyance.

In the year before the accession of Queen Elizabeth – on 28 June 1557 – there occurred the birth of one of the most attractive and interesting of all the members of the Howard family, particularly from the point of view of the family's religious history. The man in question was Philip Howard, eldest son of the 4th Duke of Norfolk; he was subsequently canonised as a saint.

Brought up an Anglican, he became wilful and selfish in his late teens; but by 1580, having inherited the earldom of Arundel and taken on its attendant responsibilities, he soon exhibited a new seriousness. One day he was pacing up and down the long gallery of Arundel Castle, a room which still survives and is now refitted as the library. 'After a long and great conflict within himself,' as his biographer reports, he decided to become a practising Catholic, following the example of his wife, most of his family and many distinguished English aristocrats at this time. The 'Counter-Reformation' was beginning. As John Martin Robinson puts it: 'These were the heroic years of English recusancy; the period of priests in hiding ... escapes, captures, triumphs and tragedies, which even now, after four centuries, sheds a certain romantic glamour over the English Catholics.'

The Norfolks were very much part of this glamorous panorama, the

two most outstanding periods being the reign of Queen Elizabeth I and
the Victorian era. The newly converted earl, now that the blunder of
the vindictive papal condemnation of 1570 had brought such danger
and damage to English Catholics, decided to ship out of England and
quietly practise his faith abroad. His changed demeanour, however, and
obvious reluctance, though a courtier, to observe the prescribed Anglican observances, had attracted suspicion; he was betrayed, arrested on
the high seas, brought back to England and committed to the Tower on
25 April 1585. The machinery for judicial murder, by now familiar in
Tudor England, was put in motion, and he was condemned to remain
imprisoned during the 'Queen's pleasure'. His demeanour while in the
Tower was heroic and accompanied by heavy self-inflicted austerities.
Even his 'enemies' admired and came to love him. At length, in April
1589, he was brought to trial, the principal charge against him being
that he had prayed for the success of the Spanish Armada. A mass of
defective evidence was brought against him until, finally, the desired
guilty verdict was achieved. He was consequently condemned to death.
J. M. Robinson's comment refers to it as 'the only case in English legal
history where somebody has been condemned a traitor for *praying* for
something to come about'. Philip's behaviour, however, had so amaz-
ing an effect on all who witnessed it that his execution was delayed. The
Queen could not, at first, bring herself to sign his death warrant.

The abeyance of the Norfolk dukedom lasted from the execution
Philip became seriously ill and his condition while in prison gradually worsened; but the maintenance of the new Establishment, as
masterminded by Burghley for the Queen, required that his life must be
sacrificed. This was duly done with the maximum retributive cruelty, in
order to make the necessary exhibition of the saintly Earl, who
compounded his guilt in official eyes by his rejection of the Court and
all it stood for. This affront to Burghley's pride was, in the end, Philip
Arundel's greatest offence. To many others he transmitted an irresistible
and lasting appeal, so that by his saintly and heroic death in the Tower,
his was the final victory. He was canonised by Pope Paul VI in 1970 at
a ceremony attended by his family, and is now enshrined in Arundel
Cathedral of which he is the titular saint.

The abeyance of the Norfolk dukedom lasted from the execution
of the 4th Duke in 1572 until 1660; and it was not until more than
a hundred years after the restoration of the title that the family, apart
from isolated interventions and successes, had any appreciable effect

on English Catholic life. The penal years, after all, were long and dark for English Catholics – condemned as they were as unwilling traitors having originally been encouraged by the Pope to depose their sovereign.

The seventeenth century saw some slight amelioration in English fortunes for various reasons and for the Howards it was made notable by the spectacular career of yet another Philip Howard. He was born in 1629 and decided to become a Dominican friar at the age of sixteen while travelling in Italy. He was ordained to the priesthood in 1652 at the early age of twenty-three. In May 1660 he accompanied the restored King Charles II to England and was subsequently appointed Chaplain to the Catholic Queen Catherine of Braganza.

His zealous Catholic activities were at first tolerated but later became dangerous. He left England under a cloud but was rewarded in 1675 by Pope Clement X with the Cardinal's hat as a reward for his zeal and a recompense for his exile. The rest of his life was spent in Rome where his most notable achievement was to re-establish the Venerable English College. By now, in Macaulay's words, Philip Howard was 'the Chief Counsellor of the Holy See in matters relating to his country'. Unfortunately he was powerless to mitigate, though he disapproved of the tactless and heavy-handed efforts of the Catholic King James II to restore the ancient faith in England.

Cardinal Norfolk lived to see his life's ambition realised when the English Dominican Province was revived in 1674 with himself as first Vicar-General. He died three weeks later, at the age of sixty-four.

In the eighteenth century nearly all the members of the Howard family entered religion and lived abroad as nuns or priests. In each generation only one son married and carried on the line. When at last the whole 'paraphernalia' (J. M. Robinson's word) of anti-Catholic discrimination was swept away in 1829, the result as far as the Norfolks were concerned was almost an anti-climax, but it inaugurated a chapter of family history which was to end in a glow of justifiable satisfaction, even a blaze of glory.

For obvious reasons this phase was of dominant interest to Miles as well as being the principal inspiration for his role as England's leading layman. Significantly, too, the period in question was ushered in by the inheritance, in 1815, of the dukedom by the Glossop Howards, i.e. Miles's immediate forebears. Members of this branch of the family have been its most consistently and strongly Catholic ones, being the descendants of Thomas, the 14th Earl of Arundel. He it was who petitioned in vain for the restoration to the Howards of the dukedom of Norfolk, but was created Earl of Norfolk thus keeping the Norfolk title in the Howard family. When in 1815 his direct descendant Bernard became 12th Duke, there was a dramatic upsurge of Catholic involvement which was in keeping with the unbroken religious loyalty, for the next hundred and fifty years, of this branch of the family.

The nineteenth century indeed was a glittering period in the history of the Dukes of Norfolk as English Catholic leaders. 'Duke Henry', creator of the modern Arundel Castle, is generally considered to be the most outstanding of them; and in terms of grandiose gestures and generous benefactions, it can be truthfully said that he was.

When a fuller history of all this comes to be written, however, it may well be that, in terms of actual effectiveness to the world around him, the dukedom of Miles himself will be seen as the most important of all. The second Elizabethan age will thus recall some of the dramas of the first, if for very different reasons. In the first Elizabethan age the Pope condemned the Queen, in the second he paid a state visit to England.

Though immensely proud of his family's heroism during the worst of the 'penal days', Miles had an awareness, not shared by all Roman Catholics, of the vital distinction between execution for heresy – as in the time of the Catholic Queen Mary – and execution for treason, as in the time of the Protestant Queen Elizabeth.

This awareness had a direct connection with the fact that in 1570 Pope Pius V excommunicated Queen Elizabeth I and purportedly released her Catholic subjects from their allegiance to her. He thus condemned all English Catholics to be, henceforth, traitors to their Queen if they conspired (as he wished them to) in any way to effect the restoration of England to Catholicism. Allied as he was to England's greatest enemy, the Spain of Philip II, the Pope's action was equivalent to a declaration of war. Indeed one of its eventual effects was an attempted invasion of England with the sending of the Spanish Armada in 1588. Meanwhile, a Catholic 'fifth column' operated within England. The resulting conspirators, quite a lot of them Jesuits, engaged in continuous subversive activity and, in many cases, were arrested and executed – for treason. In English Catholic folklore, they rank as heroic martyrs for the faith. Heroic they certainly were, but they need never have died. With certain exceptions, Catholics and Protestants, by exercising discretion and in dignified comradeship, had co-existed happily in Elizabethan England prior to the papal condemnation of 1570. After that there was a disastrous series of Catholic plots, ruthlessly repressed by Lord Burghley and Walsingham on behalf of the Queen.

Finally, but only very much later, there came, for English Catholicism, what Sir Shane Leslie called the 'Second Spring'. In the late eighteenth century certain of the disabilities against Roman Catholics in England were lifted. But it was not until 1829 that full 'Catholic Emancipation' was achieved. This big step forward had been the prime objective in the life of Bernard, 12th Duke of Norfolk. And as soon as possible after the necessary enabling Act of Parliament was passed, he was able to take his seat in the Lords, the first Catholic member of the family to sit there since the 6th Duke had withdrawn in 1678. In the same year (1829) his son Henry, later 13th Duke, became the first (openly avowed) Catholic to sit as an MP. He held his seat until summoned to the Upper House as Lord Maltravers in 1841, succeeding to the dukedom in the following year.

A brief mention must be made here of a descendant of the Howards (not through an eldest son), namely Charles Edward, Cardinal Howard, the great-nephew of Bernard the 12th Duke, born in the same year as Catholic Emancipation (1829). He was the other member of the family to become a Cardinal and though never reaching such exalted heights in that capacity as his predecessor, he played an important part in the Howard (and general English) Catholic Revival. He went off to Rome to become a priest after a worldly youth in the Life Guards, and spent some time as a missionary in India. He returned to Rome to become a central figure, with particular regard to English Catholic affairs, being finally elevated to the rank of Cardinal in 1877. He died in 1892 and was buried with elaborate canonical honours at Arundel. His life thus overlapped that of the three ducal descendants of the aforementioned Bernard, 12th Duke, all of them called Henry and all important in the Norfolks' Catholic surge in the nineteenth and early twentieth centuries.[4]

4 Their story is a fascinating one and its details can be read in J. M. Robinson's history of the Dukes of Norfolk, the 'curtain-raiser' being the eventful life of Bernard the 12th Duke (see J. M. Robinson, *op.cit.*, pp. 189–237).

Miles's immediate predecessor, another Bernard, succeeded as a minor in 1917. After the Second World War, Miles became clear heir through the second son of the 13th Duke of Norfolk, who had been created 1st Lord Howard of Glossop. Inheriting the dukedom in 1975, he held the position, with its attendant responsibilities, for twenty-seven years. The quincentenary of the Norfolk dukedom in 1983 was celebrated by a memorable ecumenical service in the Tower of London followed by a dinner for 200 members of the Howard family at the Fishmongers' Hall (Miles was a past Prime Warden).

2
Arundel

The first point to be made regarding Arundel is that, effectively, Miles saved the castle and all that it symbolised as the seat of the dukedom and as a treasure house of national importance. This was one of his most notable achievements and a significant demonstration of his effective mixture of abilities. He was a shrewd strategist and engaged in a fruitful and friendly cooperation with a wide variety of people – accountants, museum directors, lawyers, government officials, and many others.

Miles and his father had agreed with Bernard that the castle should go to the National Trust sometime in the 1950s or 1960s. The National Trust, however, was a very different organisation at that time from what it has since become. It was thus agreed that, as an alternative, Arundel could be vested in an independent charitable trust. This is what Bernard originally wanted, but the plan was turned down by Parliament in 1956.

Miles, by 1975, was determined that the castle should not go to the National Trust but that the family connection and tradition should continue. He wanted his elder son Eddie to live there and be squire of Arundel when he grew up and married. Through Lord Donaldson in the House of Lords he learned that new legislation – allowing heritage trusts for the public benefit – would now make this original 1950s' project possible. He set up Arundel Castle Trustees Limited with himself as chairman – one of the first trusts of its kind in England and now copied by many other great houses, e.g. Chatsworth, Harewood, Wilton, etc.

The castle itself, the Fitzalan chapel (the family chapel within a sizeable church standing in the grounds) and the family mausoleum have been extensively restored since 1966, at the cost of over a million pounds. Following the breaking of the entail by Act of Parliament in 1956, the estates were divided between the families of Miles and Bernard, the latter having had four daughters but no son.

The new arrangements worked extremely well, largely thanks to the active support of Miles. He kept an office at Arundel and visited it at least once a week until within a couple of years of his death.

Arundel Castle, apart from anything else, is home to many priceless treasures, owing a lot to the so-called 'Collector Earl'. He was Thomas the 14th Earl of Arundel, the only son of St Philip Howard. He was the doyen of the early English private collectors, and one of the most prominent of the 'Howard Earls' who were active during the years (1572–1660) when the dukedom of Norfolk was in abeyance. When Thomas was restored in blood as Earl of Arundel and Surrey in 1604, he was granted Arundel Castle and the rest of the Norfolk estates. From this time onwards, therefore, the castle began its existence as the store-house of its many priceless possessions, although Thomas's first love as the showpiece for his collecting genius was Arundel House in London.

The building, a hundred years after the reconstruction by the 15th Duke in 1875–1900 in Gothic Revival taste, needed a lot of attention. Thanks to Miles, it is now in first rate condition, the roof and fabric repaired, rewiring nearly completed; as for the contents, pictures and furniture have been restored and archives catalogued. Miles was personally responsible for all this, giving more than merely nominal support. He personally planned and managed it all.

He inherited all the contents of Arundel which were entailed with the dukedom. The major chattels were exempt from death duties on the grounds of historical and artistic importance; but the lesser contents unfortunately attracted a large tax bill.

Miles pioneered an ingenious way of meeting this without selling things or breaking up the collection. After patient negotiations he gave five important portraits in lieu of tax to the National Portrait Gallery on condition that they remained on display at Arundel. This was the first time that such a thing had happened at a non-National Trust house and again set an important precedent copied elsewhere, much to the benefit of the visiting public which prefers to see things in their histori-cal context.

Miles was also responsible for many innovations at Arundel, among them a shop and a restaurant. He inaugurated the annual Arundel Festival which takes place during a week in August every year. This was originally the idea of his actress daughter Marsha. It includes the production of an outdoor Shakespeare history play, until recently run by Judy Buckland. Miles gave much invaluable help through his contacts with sponsors. The whole concept continues to flourish.

At first, Miles ran the home farm and the shoot, but gradually handed over all the estate side to Eddie, who lives with his family in the east wing. Lavinia (Norfolk) had meanwhile gone to live in Park House, remaining Lord Lieutenant of Sussex.

Although Miles never actually lived at the castle, he would stay there quite often, paying a fee for so doing for himself and his guests. There was one occasion which he always particularly enjoyed, and this was the annual celebration, beginning at the Cathedral and ending at the castle, in connection with the popular Catholic feast of Corpus Christi. The date of this feast day is variable, but it is always celebrated on the Thursday after Trinity Sunday.

For psychological, even more than theological, reasons the annual elaborate celebration of Corpus Christi at Arundel was highly appropriate to recent Howard history. The Solemn Mass in the Cathedral would be followed by processing over the carpet of flowers down the aisle, up through the castle grounds, and finishing with benediction in the quadrangle. Afterwards there would be a dinner attended by both visitors and friends, enlivened by Miles's generous hospitality.

The liturgical side of these celebrations was formerly presided over by the Bishop of Arundel and Brighton, Cormac Murphy O'Connor, a close friend of Miles. Bishop Cormac's subsequent appointment as Cardinal, Archbishop of Westminster, gave immense satisfaction to Miles, as well as to the Catholics of England and Wales as a whole, both clerical and lay. The Rt. Rev. Kieran Conry, who succeeded Cormac in the Arundel and Brighton diocese, continues to preside at Corpus Christi.

While Arundel played a centrally important part in the life of Miles, it is even truer to say that Miles played a crucial part in the continuing and flourishing life of Arundel.

3
The Years of 'Apprenticeship'

Miles left the Army on 30 September 1967. He only had a short period of relaxation before taking up his job in the City. His diary entry for 20 November of that year reads: 'I entered Robert Fleming & Co. as a clerk.'

His brother-in-law Jerry Jamieson, married to his sister Mariegold, had been a director there for some years and was partly responsible for Miles joining the firm. For all the modest implications of the diary entry, the clerk had become a director by the time of his first holiday early the following year, when he went with four of his children and the Jamiesons on a skiing trip to Verbier.

Soon after their return to England, the first fruits of Miles's advance in the company begun to appear. As of 1 April he was attached to the stockbroking section of Hoare's Bank and started to widen his experience in that direction. He was, among other things, put in charge of the investment connected with the extensive house-building operations of the Ladybridge firm at Bolton.

Later that year – in October – he was attached briefly to Alexander Brown in Baltimore. Fleming's had already spotted Miles's strong potential as an 'ambassador' as well as an operator of more run-of-the-mill or home-based activities. All of this, at least indirectly, led to Miles being put in charge of selling Eurodollars. In this he was involved for almost the whole of 1970, finally being attached to Fleming Suez under Christopher Loder (Lord Wakehurst) and Guy de la Pressle.

Whenever he was in London at this period, Miles, as he notes in his diary, often had lunch alone with his youngest brother Mark who (also an employee of Fleming's) – in Miles's own words – 'taught me so much about the City'.

In the course of 1971 Miles and Anne moved into a flat at 11/52 Pont Street, round the corner from 23 Lennox Gardens where, all too soon, his father, after the death of Mona in August, was to find himself living alone. He died in August 1972, almost exactly a year after his wife.

These two sad deaths – meaning that Miles became first Lord Beaumont and then Lord Howard of Glossop – were, of course, to change his life, though for the time being he continued his (more or less) full-time employment with Fleming's. In January 1973 he went to Jeddah and then on to Tokyo, Hong Kong, Singapore and Djakarta. His services as an 'ambassador' were becoming ever more obvious and useful, as well as providing him with valuable experience in his 'apprenticeship' for public life.

Aspects of the latter were already beginning to cast their shadow over him. Although he attended the 1973 opening of Parliament 'under Bernard' (Norfolk) it was very much a dress rehearsal for a greatly enlarged participation in future. For although he wore only a morning coat for this occasion – albeit surmounted by his Beaumont Baron's robes – this was to be the last time that his appearance and contribution were relatively subdued.

The next opening of Parliament, as it happened, was unexpectedly soon – on 12 March 1974. This was entirely organised by Miles as Bernard was too ill. He died on 31 January in the following year 1975.

All of these events meant that Miles's whole life entered a completely new dimension. Added to this, he was becoming more closely involved with Catholicism – as well as general secular and public affairs – and on 5 March that year lunched with Cardinal Heenan and had a very candid talk about the worrying situation in Northern Ireland. He was to become chairman of the Tablet Trust, running the well-known Catholic weekly, and in January 1976 attended the 'Tablet Table' dinner at the Cardinal pub in Francis Street – 'the first of many'. A new life, on several fronts, was quickly opening up. His 'apprentice years' were over.

The house that had been the principal Howard London home, 23 Lennox Gardens, was sold, but Miles and Anne decided to retain the house at the end of the area immediately behind it, the former stable. This they had refurbished, with a front door in Clabon Mews; and from January 1976 this became their London home.

4

A Rich Tradition and
a Baptism of Fire

Miles became the natural lay leader of English Catholicism as much by the intimate part played in his life from his earliest days by his Catholic faith as by the exalted position in society and public life that he assumed in his later years. Both his mother and father were what his lifelong friend Monsignor Alfred Gilbey always called 'Catholic to the marrow of their bones'. It was a proud tradition to inherit.

The Howards' Catholicism, moreover, was of a deeply pious and traditional nature, many of whose characteristics are seldom seen in England today. The Howard family, and the pageant of the Dukes of Norfolk, were steeped in English Catholic history. Miles's schooling at Ampleforth in the Twenties and Thirties blended with a life in the holidays at Carlton in a fashion that fairly breathed Catholic devotion.

To be a 'daily communicant' – i.e recipient every day of the sacrament of Holy Communion – was a cherished ideal among Catholics such as the Howards. Miles's father Bernard was an unfailing daily communicant when the family were in London. Living, as they did, in Pont Street, there was a Catholic church nearby, St Mary's, Cadogan Street, which Bernard Howard visited every day. It was his habit also to drop in at the Oratory, almost equally near, on most evenings on his way back from the City for Vespers or Benediction.

Let us look back for a moment at the world of Miles's parents, particularly at the way they practised their Catholic faith. There was, and indeed still is, a private chapel at Carlton Towers. It was just to the right of the garden entrance which always served as the front door. Mass was said every Friday morning at nine o'clock by the local priest from Carlton village who stayed for breakfast.

The chapel at Carlton was visited regularly even though there was Mass only once a week. A family rosary was recited every day, and this practice continued even after the war when I used to stay at Carlton. At about half-past six every evening, word would be discreetly passed round among the Catholic guests that family rosary would be recited in the chapel before all went up to change for dinner.

The unspoken influence on all the family – and, indirectly, on their friends – of Miles's mother Mona and her wonderful husband Bernard was plain for all to see. Had it been in any way sanctimonious, it would have lost all its effect. In fact, it was anything but that. Mona's piety was of the practical, down-to-earth type ranging from being sure the fish had been ordered for Friday, to being the extremely efficient chairman, for many years, of such organisations as the Catholic Needlework Guild.

Her husband's piety was touchingly simple and sincere. His daily attendance at Mass at St Mary's, Cadogan Street, was accompanied by an identical ritual every day. He would invariably arrive at the church at almost exactly seven minutes to eight in the morning; you could safely have set your watch by him. If there happened to be no altar boy, he would go up into the sanctuary to act as server.

This at least was his unchanging routine when in London during the late 1950s and throughout the 1960s. It continued almost up to his death in 1972. He also, during the war, paid weekly visits to the Convent of Perpetual Adoration at Tyburn to pray for his sons on active service. (Miles had been in the Grenadiers since 1937, Michael joined the Scots Guards at the outbreak of war, Martin entered the Army – also Grenadier Guards – in 1942.)

During the war, too, the Fitzalan Howards kept up their friendship with Arthur Hinsley, Cardinal Archbishop of Westminster from 1937 to 1943. He was a close personal friend of Winston Churchill, and showed unwavering patriotism throughout the war. It was an open secret that he did not agree with any sort of appeasement of Hitler.

Life had meanwhile been transformed at Carlton Towers which became a VAD centre, with Mona in charge. Miles's sister Mariegold took a uniformed role as one of the VADs, and was joined by my cousin Meg Newman. Meg, her parents having died, stayed on after the war and lived semi-permanently with the Howards, later becoming Michael's second wife. She fitted in perfectly with the very special atmosphere of Carlton which played so important a part in Miles's progress toward eventual leadership of England's Catholic laity.

Not only was Miles, all his life, a devout Catholic, but he always took a lively and well-informed interest in the Church's history, theology and effectiveness, especially as far as England was concerned. His involvement naturally became much greater after he inherited the dukedom early in 1975. Indeed this turned out to be a very important year in English Catholic history as a whole, in which Miles played a highly significant part. Until that time he had deliberately taken a back seat in Catholic affairs but almost immediately he was inundated with invitations and requests to be involved, as president, chairman, patron, or in some other capacity, in one of the many Catholic societies or charities of England and Wales. One of the first posts to which he was elected was the important one of President of the Catholic Union of Great Britain. This is the country's most significant lay society and is officially described as 'a non-political association of members of the Catholic laity to watch over Catholic interests, whenever possible in concert with other Christians and others of like mind, especially in matters arising from Government action, proposed legislation or the activities of local authorities and other public bodies'.

I happened to be on the Executive of the Catholic Union myself at the time when Miles first became President and it is true to say that his advent produced a welcome breath of fresh air. He sometimes chaired the meetings which, at that time, were held in the Challoner Club in Pont Street. He was the ideal chairman. His military efficiency saw to it that business was dispatched smoothly and briskly, but his unfailing courtesy and attention to detail ensured that all points of view were given adequate opportunity for expression.

Miles's flat at this time was on the opposite side of Pont Street, and he often asked me to come over and have a drink after the meeting. We would usually be joined by some of the other members of the Union Executive and a lively discussion invariably ensued. I particularly remember Miles's disarming modesty on such occasions. 'I'm only a new boy in these Catholic matters,' he would say. 'It's up to you lot to put me on the right track.' Miles, in his strikingly – almost alarming – disarming way would say things like 'What are our bishops like? Are they good chaps? I've never met Cardinal Heenan for example. Is he a good man?'

It so happened that I knew John Heenan well. I very much liked and admired him. His years as Archbishop of Westminster (1965–75) were important but, in many ways, frustrating ones, especially for him.

These were the years following the Vatican Council (1961–64) which had produced, at every level, so startlingly different an outlook and atmosphere in the Church. They were also the years following the prolonged sitting of the unprecedentedly large and international commission called to consider and report on representative opinion throughout the Church on the vexed question of the morality of birth control. The question came to be a very important one for Miles not very long after his inheriting the dukedom.

Cardinal Heenan had been a vice-president of the massive Birth Control Commission, and when it had finished the exhaustive deliberations in 1966, he had returned to England from Rome confident that the Pope, in accordance with the expert advice given to him with which he agreed, would announce a change in the ruling up to that point that any form of artificial contraception was intrinsically immoral and a grave sin. But the delay in the making of any official statement dragged on for two and a half years, despite the opinion of the overwhelming majority of the Commission, and indeed of the Church, that a change was essential. This they duly reported. A different view, however, was taken by a minority, who issued their own report.

The minority report (favouring no changes in the existing ban on artificial contraception) laid much stress on the Catholic Church's claim to the exclusive guidance of the Holy Spirit in disputed matters. It argued that for the Church to be seen as changing its mind on licitness of contraception would damage this apparent possession of a monopoly of divine truth. It recalled that the Lambeth Conference of the Anglican Church had, in 1930, discussed this very matter occasioning a Papal Encyclical by way of reply. For the Anglicans had declared that birth control, by whatever method, must be a matter of conscience. Pius XI, in reply, had issued his letter *Casti Conubii*, stating that it was the (Roman) Catholic Church 'to whom God has entrusted the defence of the integrity and purity of morals ... In token of her divine ambassadorship ... And through our mouth.' The authors of the Papal Birth Control Commission's minority report were therefore horrified at any possibility of a shifting of ground, if it was 'now to be admitted that the Church erred in this her work, and that the Holy Spirit rather assists the Anglican Church'. Perish the thought!

On 18 October 1967, however, at a 'moment of historical significance' 3,000 delegates to the World Congress of the Lay Apostolate meeting in Rome had made a bold and direct challenge to the Pope. They called, in terms that were measured and yet so unambiguous as to be sensational, for revision of past Church teaching on birth control so that Catholics could in future follow their own consciences in selecting the means whereby they might limit their families. This call was coupled with certain radical pleas for the Church to be more vitally concerned in the field of world development. At the end of July, the bombshell of *Humanae Vitae* exploded. The document was dated 25 July, Feast of St James the Apostle. The operative words of this most famous of all modern Papal 'letters' came in its paragraph 11 and stated that 'every marriage act must remain open to life'. The next paragraph insisted that the 'unitive meaning and the procreative meaning' of marriage are inseparable. No artificial means may be allowed to come between these two 'meanings'. Contraception in other words could only be lawfully avoided by use of 'rhythm', a method unknown to Catholics in underdeveloped areas and elsewhere primarily available only to those with enough time and leisure to make it work. (Thoughts on the desirability of the so-called 'rhythm method' became, as will be seen, very important in the case of a widely reported incident involving Miles.)

The Catholic world was stunned and confused. Authoritative clarification was obviously needed. On 6 December Cardinal Heenan was interviewed on television by David Frost and said 'The teaching of the Church is very clear. A man is bound to follow his conscience and this is true even if his conscience is in error.' David Frost then asked, 'And if they go to their priests and say that they're doing precisely that, what should the priest say?' The Archbishop replied 'God bless you! If they're really following their conscience in the sight of God, which is all that matters – the priest, the bishop, the Pope doesn't matter compared with God.' This virtually clinched the matter. The leading English Catholic churchman had been seen and heard by millions of viewers and his opinion became public knowledge. No amount of qualifications or carefully worded statements from hierarchies could have had any comparable impact. There are still, it is true, those who like to persuade themselves that the Cardinal did not really mean what he said. Such an erroneous attitude, as he told me himself, greatly irritated him.

Miles, in years to come, often referred to those words of Cardinal Heenan. He had long been anxiously concerned about the 1968 ruling on birth control and its effect on ordinary Catholics, but it was only after 1975 that he himself became publicly involved in the controversy after becoming Duke of Norfolk. (Coincidentally, David Frost had become his son-in-law, having married his second daughter, Carina.) At one of those discussions at his flat in Pont Street, moreover, several of us urged Miles – the self-styled 'new boy' in the role of Catholic leader – to lose no time in getting to know the Cardinal. It was only his reticence to take a lead in Catholic affairs up until 1975, and his diffident acceptance of his new role as duke, that had delayed him becoming a close friend and confidant of the Cardinal and other members of the hierarchy.

Indeed there was a particular reason for his so doing, as the Cardinal's state of health was giving cause for alarm. Within a short time, to everyone's satisfaction, Miles and John Heenan had become close friends and allies. Each admired the other's rock-like faith combined with an honest determination, as Miles put it, to 'call a spade a bloody shovel'.

No sooner, however, was their friendship blossoming and deepening when, that very autumn (1975), the Cardinal's health took a sudden turn for the worse. His illness became common knowledge and he died on 7 November. Sadly though he was missed, the Church, it has been said without cynicism, must keep operating regardless of personal tragedy and loss. Steps for the appointment of a new Archbishop of Westminster moved ahead rapidly.

Quite soon afterwards, I was at a meeting of the Catholic Union Executive chaired by Miles, after which he asked me to come across the street for a drink, since a long-time friend of his and mine, Father Michael Hollings, would also be coming. Conversation, not unnaturally, quickly turned to the burning topic of the moment, namely who the next Archbishop of Westminster would – or perhaps should – be. Miles turned to Father Hollings and said 'You'd be the best chap, Michael.' 'Out of the question, Miles!' he said immediately and we both had to agree with this verdict.

Miles got up to replenish our drinks and I remember hearing myself saying: 'What a pity it can't be someone like Basil Hume.' It was then that Michael said: 'If Basil Hume is to get it, there is only one person to pave the way. And that's you, Miles.' Miles exclaimed 'I say, chaps, now look here… Steady on!' Nevertheless…

To cut a long story short, Miles rang up the Apostolic Delegate's Secretary the next day and went to see the Delegate himself, Archbishop Bruno Heim, the day after. Miles went straight to the point in mentioning Basil. All of this happened in late January 1976. Events thereafter moved fairly rapidly by Church standards and in early March it was announced that a press conference would be held at the Press Club, then in Shoe Lane, near Fleet Street, at which the name of the new Archbishop of Westminster would be announced. A slip of paper was circulated on which was written the name of Abbot Basil Hume, OSB.

5
Catholic Union ... and Beyond

Miles, as mentioned in the last chapter, became President of the Catholic Union of Great Britain shortly after inheriting the dukedom. I have already quoted Miles as describing himself a 'new boy' in Catholic affairs at this time. He was thus grateful for any help and advice he could get, and this he received, from no one more importantly than someone who became a close friend of Miles, namely Philip Daniel. This was particularly true with regard to the Catholic Union where Philip was a key figure for many years. Tragically, Philip died in early 2004.

When working on this book about Miles, I naturally contacted Philip and we had a most interesting lunch at which Miles was the chief topic of conversation. Subsequently he sent me a copy of his booklet *For the Common Good*, which is an account of the work of the Catholic Union of Great Britain from 1975 to 1997.

He also, most kindly, sent me his own personal appreciation and memories of Miles, whom he had come to like and admire so much in the course of their years of work together. I feel it would be best, therefore, in taking forward this part of Miles's story, to do so in Philip's own words, as they give such an excellent picture of Miles's extremely valuable contribution to the work of the Catholic Union. In the year after his becoming President, for example, he kindly allowed Arundel Castle to be the venue for a Union garden party. It put the seal on the beginning of what became, thanks to Miles, truly a new era in English Catholic affairs.

In quoting verbatim from some parts of Philip's booklet as well as reproducing in full his appreciation of Miles, the quotations from his booklet *For the Common Good* come first, followed by the appreciation.

1975 was a very significant year in the history of the Catholic Union. Miles Fitzalan Howard had become 17th Duke of Norfolk in succession to his cousin, Bernard, the 16th Duke. Cardinal Heenan, the 8th Archbishop of Westminster, died in November just before the Union's first Annual General Meeting under the chairmanship of the new Duke and was succeeded by Dom Basil Hume, a monk and former Head of Ampleforth College. The Union had come into existence under the Presidency of Henry, the 15th Duke, in 1872 as a result of a direct suggestion by Archbishop Manning that a prestigious and responsible but entirely lay body was needed to take upon itself the direct representation to the public authorities of the rightful needs and aspirations of the growing Catholic electorate.

It was Miles's Presidency of the Union that firmly established him as England's leading Catholic layman, a position held with dignity and courtesy. Working closely with Miles at all times was this same Philip Daniel whose personal appreciation continues as follows:

Miles Fitzalan Howard, the 17th Duke of Norfolk, may well be the last of his line, not of Dukes of Norfolk as such because he is well supported by heirs, but as being a 'leader' of the Catholics of England and Wales by birth and social position. He embraced, or endured it with a self-sacrificing willingness to acknowledge an obligation, which he had no intention to evade.

Miles, his name so aptly chosen, was truly a soldier, and has that good soldier's attribute of transparent honesty and a directness that can be utterly disarming. Confronted at an early stage of his succession to Duke Bernard as Earl Marshal with the 'leadership' of the visible Catholic presence in Parliament and with it 'the Establishment', his answer was swift and memorable. 'Very good,' he said, 'but if you want me to do the job, I want to know why, and how you propose to support me by doing the real donkey work yourselves; a general's no good without a loyal army.'

In the tussles in the Committee rooms, and in influential gatherings and broadsheet interventions outside Parliament on such matters as educational administration, data protection, the nationality and immigration laws, mental health and criminal justice, human fertilisation and embryo research, and the increasingly baleful effect of the abortion business, the person of the 'good Duke' was a rock around which others gathered whenever the seas seemed stormy. A Liberal democrat peeress remarked in a meeting where she was not meant to be quoted: 'Miles Norfolk's lot is always good for 50 votes.'

In the new dispensation whatever be the form of the House of Lords which finally emerges, it is unlikely that an essentially non-party figure, such as Miles, will be able to rally a distinct and coherent body of followers of sufficient a size to make a real difference to business in the way the Catholic 'rump' has been able to do.

As Mark Bence-Jones wrote in his book on *The Catholic Families*, there was a time around 1829 when it became 'fashionable to be a Catholic'. Those times have long gone, but in the second half of the last century there was a strong and discernible Catholic influence, inspired by Vatican II, in the non-elected part of Parliament, at the centre of which for twenty-seven years was Miles.

6

A Public Profile

From the point of view of being a standard-bearer Miles's first year as duke was, as we have seen, something of a baptism of fire. Thereafter, the Catholic Union provided a stout umbrella for his Catholic leadership activities. Otherwise he was largely on his own in championing Catholic causes and finding himself the target of controversy. As far as the House of Lords was concerned, he became an articulate advocate of matters of Catholic (and general) concern, but he did not become a regular participant in debates until after 1981.

His approach to Catholic affairs was very much a part of his approach to all the other new aspects of his life on becoming a duke. The public got some idea of what this was as a result of a televised interview at Bacres, his house near Henley-on-Thames, on 1 February 1975. He was not asked any questions about religion – but gave, by one answer, some idea of how he would face up to controversial matters. No one would ever have suspected that he had once been known by his friends as a generally shy and retiring young man. His thirty years in getting to know the world as a Grenadier had changed all that.

'One of the things about being in the Army is that you can't be shy,' he said. 'You learn that you've got to speak up or you're lost... I've been chased around by drill sergeants so much that I've lost any fear.'

Another attribute gained from his life as a soldier was efficiency. This was much in evidence, soon after he had become Duke of Norfolk, in the course of one of the most high-profile and successful Catholic occasions to occur in England for a long time. Actually the main organiser of the event was Anne. But it was a good example of that close cooperation with which they went about all their joint activities.

They were now in constant demand to take a prominent part in any and every important Catholic public project simply because of who they were; but another vital element was their infectious willingness to participate. It was therefore no surprise that Miles became centrally involved with the affairs of Westminster Cathedral, an involvement that became even more active after the consecration of Basil Hume as Archbishop. Plans for a special event in the Cathedral, connected with the 1977 celebration of the Queen's Silver Jubilee year, began to take shape soon after Miles's inheritance of the dukedom.

One of the themes of the year was to be flowers. More than 4,000 amateur flower arrangers were to organise floral decorations in churches all over the country on Sunday, 5 June. And on 30 June, the day of the Queen's first London tour, a flower arrangers' 'Chelsea' was to be held at Westminster Cathedral, continuing until 3 July.

The event was to be known as the International Festival of Flowers and Music, and the President was to be the Duchess of Norfolk. Regarding the display at Westminster Cathedral, Anne told Paula Davies of the *Daily Telegraph* (9 April 1977) that 'every square inch of that huge edifice will be ablaze with flowers'. India was sending its own florist to arrange Himalayan flowers, while the Japanese would be contributing their own delicate art of Ikebana.

The event at the Cathedral would be part of an ongoing campaign to raise £1 million for the Westminster Cathedral Appeal of which Miles was chairman. Anne reported that £730,000 had already been raised, adding that 'As one of the great churches of London, its preservation has a national and ecumenical appeal.'

The occasion attracted widespread publicity and had the effect of letting more people know something about Anne. As an Army wife she had needed to become an efficient organiser, coping with constant moves; and all her children – now aged between fifteen and twenty-six – had been born during this period. None of the births had been without anxiety, but each was characteristically connected – throughout the family – with prayer for a safe delivery and continued health.

With Miles now retired from the Army, there was more time to enjoy life at Bacres. Part of the pleasure of living there was the scope it gave Anne as a gardener, although the impressive flint and brick walled garden was very much a 'do-it-yourself' joint enterprise. Roses were the favourite flowers of both of them.

Now, because of the Festival, Anne's skills were being called on for something on a spectacular scale, and she was going to need all her talents for organisation. The committee she was obliged to form was to oversee the organisation of the Flower Festival. Yet, ironically, 'I'm terrified of committees and all the performance that goes with them,' she was quoted as saying at the time. 'It's far better to get a few people together and then get on with it.'

The whole event was extremely impressive. It was also a financial success, with two beneficiaries: the Queen's Jubilee Fund and the Westminster Cathedral Appeal. The latter, under Miles's presidency, continued to benefit from an ongoing fund-raising programme in which Miles took a vigorous part with the Friends of Westminster Cathedral.

There was one occasion, in 1979, when Miles was faced with a clash of commitments between his activities on behalf of the Westminster Cathedral Appeal and his responsibilities as Earl Marshal. He and Anne were due on a month-long fund-raising mission to the United States. With all the arrangements in place, their plans were overtaken by the fall of the Labour Government, a general election and the requirement for Miles to be present at the State Opening of Parliament on 15 May – right in the middle of their tour. There was nothing for it but to allow for a three-day break during their itinerary around the States. This was accordingly arranged, and on May 14 they flew back to England. Miles duly presided at the State Opening of Parliament on the 15th; and the next day they flew back to New York to continue their fund-raising mission, which was a resounding success. By the time their trip was over, many thousands of Americans had heard about the needs of London's Roman Catholic Cathedral and its '12 million bricks', and had contributed with their customary generosity.

1979 was a busy year for other reasons, one in particular. Anne was president of yet another floral festival to take place in Westminster Cathedral, this time in connection with the International Year of the Child. It was to last from 12 July until 15 July and was to be visited by Her Majesty the Queen. On 20 July the *Catholic Herald* contained a distinctive account of the Queen's visit from the pen of Patrick O'Donovan.

The visit of the Queen last Friday to Westminster Cathedral went curiously unreported. I suspect, though I do not know, that this was intentional.

Well it was, I suppose, a potentially difficult or even embarrassing occasion. We know that Charles II was received on his protracted death scene into the Catholic Church. James II, his thick brother, was a loyal, if sinful Catholic and since then no British reigning monarch has ever attended a Catholic service.

It is true that Queen Victoria went into the church at Chisle-
hurst to lay flowers on the coffin of the Prince Imperial, the son of
the Emperor Napoleon III. He had been speared to death in the
British army by Zulus in Africa

There is a persistent Catholic myth that Edward VII was
received into the church on his death bed. Apart from the fact that
he used to go to largely Catholic countries to take the waters,
there is absolutely no truth in this.

Westminster Cathedral was looking rather special. Indeed it
was pure delight. The high altar was made into a great towering
hillock out of which the vaguely Byzantine crucifix grew. There
was a vast mass of roses on Cardinal Heenan's grave and the
candles were burning in Cardinal Vaughan's little chapel.

The occasion was joyous and beautiful and good, and a decent
use for one of the major masterpiece buildings of London.

There was an extraordinary moment when the Cardinal stood
quite alone at the front door of his Cathedral, more plainly
dressed than his predecessors, facing a crowded and friendly
piazza – full of people. It was, on a vast scale, like a confident
priest in his parish waiting for the Mayor. It was superbly
unpompous. And then he came back with the Queen and the
Duke and her little personal court. Marvellously – no fuss. The
Cathedral was packed to its enormous gills. The nobility stood
under the great organ and quietly and perfectly from far away on
the High Altar the choir sang 'God Save the Queen'.

The Cardinal took the Queen round a corona of clergy. Then
the Duchess of Norfolk led the Queen and the Duke down the
right hand aisle past chapel after chapel, crammed with flowers,
introducing the ladies who had denuded gardens and heaped up
the blossoms. With no notebook in her hand, she remembered
them all. It could not have been more relaxed.

It was nice to recall that the Duchess was a direct descendant of
Chancellor Thomas More and the Duke of four executed ancestors – all for putative offences against the Crown. That is now a
matter for pride, not grievance.

The Cathedral was packed. The people clapped politely. They
stood on chairs to see the Queen and the Cardinal wander past.

The flowers? Among them was a row of contrived trees along

the central aisle. They were totally formal, made of white flowers in a rich ball on a high stem. There was also an 'Arundel Cathedral Carpet' at the end of the aisle of live flowers laid in patterns on the ground.

Anne's organisational skills stood her in good stead and she was to go on to found an important national charitable organisation herself, Help the Hospices. Miles was significantly on hand – he once jokingly said he had been thinking of starting a subsidiary charity called Help the Helpers.

It all started with an invitation by a doctor friend in 1981 to visit St Joseph's Hospice in Hackney, the largest and one of the earliest of, at that time, some eighty hospices in Britain caring for the terminally ill and their families. Anne was so overwhelmed by the spirit of care and compassion that she agreed to head a campaign to raise over a million pounds for a new Residential Training Wing to train doctors and nurses in hospice and palliative care from all over the world as well as at home. Her commitment developed into an absorbing and highly successful career.

St Joseph's was founded in 1905 by the Sisters of Charity. It was among the early hospices which pioneered the concept of community-based hospice or 'palliative' care and this has been refined and improved ever since. Help the Hospices, as a national charity, was set up by Anne in 1984 to provide support and leadership to all hospices caring for patients mainly with cancer, and increasingly with other life-threatening conditions too.

Though the movement has flourished, fund-raising – despite a measure of state support – has been a constant preoccupation for the 200 independent locally-based voluntary hospices which provide, without any charge for their services, most of the care available in the movement as a whole.

Anne's life was, quite literally, transformed by these developments, in which Miles also became closely involved, making speeches and representations in the House of Lords regarding hospice care. The whole effort led to a sunny relationship between Anne, Miles and Diana Princess of Wales, who, with the Prince, was present at one of the charity's most successful fund-raising events in 1992.

In many of his diary entries, Miles mentions various occasions devoted to fund-raising for Help the Hospices. These included receptions and concerts at such venues as the Banqueting House, the Guildhall, and St John's, Smith Square. There was a special presentation of *Camelot* at the Dominion, Victoria; and a charity performance of *High Society* at the New Victoria in 1985 (where the ushers were recruited from the cast of 'East Enders').

One of the ways by which Anne personally raises money for her charity is to organise the sale of Christmas and greetings cards which feature her own paintings. She also sells her pictures at exhibitions every two or three years at a London venue.

In 1982 the Pope visited England, a happening which would have been considered impossible some years earlier. When his Alitalia Boeing 727 touched down on the tarmac at Gatwick at precisely 8 a.m. on 8 May, he was greeted by no less than 2,500 Roman Catholics chosen by ballot from the surrounding diocese of Arundel and Brighton.

The group waiting in front, the first to greet the Pope, was headed by Miles, present for the occasion in two capacities. First and foremost he was there to welcome His Holiness to Britain as the Representative of Her Majesty the Queen. He was also greeting the Pope on behalf of all the Catholics of Britain as their acknowledged leader.

Also among the welcoming party were Cardinal Basil Hume, Archbishop of Westminster, Archbishop Bruno Heim, the Apostolic Delegate, and the Anglican Bishops of Guildford and Chichester.

The Papal visit nearly did not occur at all. The war against Argentina over the Falklands was still being fought, and intense diplomatic activity at both national and ecclesiastical level had taken place before the visit went ahead. The Pope even mentioned this in the course of his speech at Gatwick.

The main thrust of the Pope's remarks was to express his pleasure of being in England on what he called his 'journey of peace'. He thanked the Duke of Norfolk and the Cardinal, and said how much he had been looking forward to the occasion 'with joyful anticipation'. He laid special stress on the ecumenical nature of his visit, a subject near to the heart of Miles. The latter's enthusiasm for closer Catholic ties with the Church of England, and other Christian churches in Britain, was based on a radical position considerably in advance of that of most of his fellow Catholics, including the clergy. He considered the official Roman

Miles as a baby with his mother, Lady Beaumont, 17 August 1915

Portrait of Miles with his mother by W. R. Symonds, 1918 (hanging at Carlton Towers)

LEFT Miles with pet rabbit Wilfred, 1925 RIGHT Miles (back, centre) in Ampleforth Corps

In class at Ampleforth

Miles (centre), Guards Armoured Division, Germany

Anne and Miles, Waikiki Beach, Honolulu, 1949

The 'watercress girl' says 'Yes'

ENGAGEMENT of society's "watercress girl," 21-year-old Miss Anne Constable Maxwell, to 33-year-old Major Miles Fitzalan Howard will be announced officially at the week-end. But she said "Yes" yesterday in Honolulu, when Major Howard flew to see her from Washington, where he is with the British Military Mission.

Miss Maxwell is the daughter of Wing Commander Maxwell, a cousin of the Duke of Norfolk. Major Howard's father is Lord Howard of Glossop.

Miss Maxwell helps to run her father's estate in Hampshire, and the top picture shows her "on duty" in the watercress beds.

Flew Pacific for a 'yes'

Miss Anne Constable Maxwell and (inset) Major Miles Fitzalan Howard.

Newspaper cuttings from the time of Miles's engagement to Anne

Anne arriving with her father for her wedding at Brompton Oratory, 4 July 1949

Miles and Anne after the service

Miles and Anne riding at the Dewey Riddle Ranch, Wyoming, September 1949

Miles and Anne riding out at the Griffins' home in Pea Pack, New Jersey, October 1949

Miles commanding the parade down the Champs Elysées during the Queen's State Visit to Paris, 5 April 1957

LEFT Miles while commanding the King's African Rifles in Nanyuki, Kenya, 1962–3
RIGHT After climbing Mount Kilimanjaro, July 1963

Miles holding Mary Queen of Scots' rosary, one of the family exhibits at Arundel Castle

Miles at the Opening of Parliament, 1980

Miles on a visit to Rome, with Pope John Paul, 1993

Anne and Miles with their family, 1994

The Queen and Miles sharing a joke at the State Opening of Parliament

Anne with Miles on his eightieth birthday at Duke Miles Wood, 1995

Four brothers wood planting: Miles, Michael, Martin, Mark

Miles, Anne and family celebrating their fiftieth wedding anniversary at
Brompton Oratory, 1999

Miles and Anne

Catholic view that Anglican priestly orders were 'null and void' to be both theologically unsound – having been overtaken by events and scholarly inquiry – as well as an insult to the Church of England. Sound scholarship, to say nothing of charity and good manners, demanded – according to Miles – an urgent and radical revision of the question.

This is not the place to describe in any detail the whole of the Pope's visit to Britain which lasted for six days. The main event took place with his visit to Canterbury. Miles and I shared a railway carriage on the journey there and talked quite a lot about Northern Ireland. We talked especially about Cardinal O'Fiach, Primate of All Ireland, whose many protests about IRA atrocities had gone unreported in the British press. I had therefore sent Miles a list of all the protests which we had compiled at the offices of the *Catholic Herald*. Miles, I remember, had been pleasantly surprised on receiving it, having liked the Cardinal when he met him. He was now worried that he might not recognise him if he happened to see him at Canterbury.

It so happened that, as we got out at Canterbury station, I was able to point out to Miles the stocky figure of the Irish Cardinal. That evening, on the way home, Miles and Cardinal O'Fiach spotted each other. 'Your Eminence!' cried Miles. 'Your Grace!' cried the Cardinal. And they fell into each other's arms.

7

The Birth Control Incident

Miles Norfolk's role as unofficial but effective leader of England's Catholics falls into three periods. The first occupies the late 1970s and early 1980s. During this period Miles was taken up, apart from his involvement with the Catholic Union of Great Britain, with largely nominal duties as president or chairman of various Catholic organisations, and as leading figure in ceremonial and national occasions. Being busy in the City limited his Catholic responsibilities.

The middle to late Eighties were somewhat different, particularly after a certain event which, almost entirely by accident, propelled him into the limelight as a Catholic of national importance to whose views people, non-Catholic and Catholic alike, listened with a new interest.

Miles had always been a well-read and well-informed Catholic, deeply devoted to his Church and faith, but distinctly having views of his own on certain matters which caused some people to suspect him of heterodoxy. Such suspicions were largely grounded in the inaccurate supposition of some Catholics that an individual's personal conscience, if sincere and well-informed, did not take priority over official Catholic teaching if there was a conflict between the two. It was over a matter ultimately concerning this very principle that, in the middle Eighties, Miles suddenly became the object of widespread interest and comment. This did not come about because of any public statement on his part. He had always been excessively discreet and careful at all times to give vent to controversial opinions only on strictly private occasions. What happened in May 1984 was purely accidental, not to say conspiratorial, but had repercussions that rumbled on for many months.

The background to the sequence of events in question has already been recounted in chapter 4 of this part, describing the aftermath of the Papal Encyclical *Humanae Vitae*, and the subsequent remarks of Cardinal Heenan. The Encyclical was published in 1968. Miles was not yet Duke of Norfolk. The controversy produced by the Papal state-ment on birth control had largely died down by the late Seventies. It burst out again, however, with a vengeance, as touching on Miles, in May 1984.

It all began with reports in various papers at the beginning of May 1984 over something said by Miles at a meeting whose proceedings he had been assured would not be made public. He felt he could therefore speak freely, as there was no danger that his words would become generally known.

Unfortunately, however, this did not happen. Typical of various reports was that which appeared in the *Guardian* on 4 May 1984. The first two paragraphs of the report were as follows:

> The Duke of Norfolk, the leading lay Roman Catholic in England, has denounced as nonsense his Church's teaching on birth control and called upon the bishops to reconsider it. His statement was disclosed last night in the transcript of a national conference held last weekend.
>
> The Duke said it was quite extraordinary that family planning was permissible in the Catholic Church by the Brook system, by the thermometer and studying your wife's periods, but you are not allowed to do it by pills or French letters or whatever.

The report went on to quote Miles's words verbatim, even though no authority had been given for such a report to appear. His exact words, as subsequently quoted, were these: 'How can you ask a married couple to do it by thermometers and what not? My wife and I did that – it didn't bloody work. How can you ask a merchant navy seaman or a miner on shift? You are asking his wife to go off with someone else .... Has everybody got to have eight children like my mother? Why have we got to be Christian Scientists over sex? That's what the Church is saying.' He also told the annual conference of the Catholic Teachers' Federation in Birmingham that he valued the fact that 'priests asked for advice, thank heavens, will say that after two or three children you can practise birth control'.

The same newspaper also reported that the Catholic Bishop of Shrewsbury was in the audience and was 'believed to have said later' that he would not have attended the meeting if he had known in advance what the duke was going to say.

The report went on to quote a 're-affirmation' by the same bishop of the Church's 'traditional teaching that marriage is sacred and the action of procreation sacramental'. (The conclusion drawn by the Church from this was – and officially still is – that any intentional frustration of birth was/is intrinsically immoral and mortally sinful.)

Also included in the *Guardian*'s report was a postscript giving a comment by a spokesman for the Catholic Teachers' Federation. He said that the Federation's members supported the traditional authoritative teachings of the Pope, the bishops and the Church on the family.

This particular paper's report of the affair was, though not intentionally, misleading in one respect. In speaking of a 'transcript' of the proceedings, it implied that some sort of semi-official recording being made somehow or another became public knowledge. The 'leak' in fact came from an unauthorised Catholic journalist whose presence was unknown to the organisers and to Miles.

The journalist in question was a reporter from the Catholic newspaper *The Universe*. This was – and is – a down-market Catholic popular tabloid that invariably took a hard-line Catholic stance on all matters of official Church teaching.

The matter was widely taken up in both the national and religious press and furiously debated for many months afterwards. Quite fortuitously, Miles's position as 'England's leading Catholic' had, overnight, assumed a totally different image. He was now a well-known centre of controversy concerning a particularly delicate field of Catholic belief, which inevitably, as a direct result, became further polarised. There were those Catholics who applauded Miles and were immensely relieved that he had 'come out' with what was, in truth, the majority view. There were others, a minority, who came to distrust Miles and no longer looked upon him as a reliable leader of Catholic opinion.

The fact that the majority and minority opinions split in this way was dramatically illustrated by what happened as a well-publicised sequel to the whole affair. An account appeared in *The Daily Telegraph* on 7 December 1984, under the by-line of Charles Laurence.

The Duke of Norfolk, Britain's premier Roman Catholic layman, last night resoundingly defeated a plan to oust him from the Presidency of the Catholic Union in the wake of his criticism of the Church's ban on contraception.

The proposal for him to step down as President and for the post to be left vacant for a year, made by a follower of the hardline *Opus Dei* organisation, was defeated by 86 votes to 4 at the Catholic Union's annual general meeting at Westminster Cathedral. Instead the Duke was re-elected for a further five years.

The vote was the culmination of a campaign against the Duke by Mr Peter Hoare, of Tunbridge Wells, following a speech by the Duke to R.C. teachers last spring in which he described the doctrine on birth control as 'nonsense'.

The Presidency of the Catholic Union, the Church's powerful lay organisation, has been held by successive Dukes of Norfolk since it was founded 105 years ago, and until last night re-election had been a formality.

After the meeting the Duke said 'I am very pleased. It is important that the freedom of speech in this Union should be maintained. People in it should be allowed to speak freely their own opinions – when they are speaking as individuals.'

In the speech to the teachers the Duke asked why Catholics, who accept such operations as that for breast cancer should be 'Christian Scientists' on sex and not allowed to use contraceptives.

The Duke, who has two sons and three daughters, did not expect the speech to be reported and declined to air his views on birth control when further pressed. 'It was meant to be a provocative address to teachers to wake them up. All doctrine should be open to discussion,' he said.

The Times's comment on Miles's intervention is worth quoting, as it was typical of non-religious media's reaction to the incident.

The Duke of Norfolk, Britain's premier Roman Catholic layman, may be about to be stripped of his Presidency of the Catholic Union following an official protest to Cardinal Hume from another Catholic group, which boasts among its members Christopher Monckton and Tory MP Sir John Biggs-Davison. *Pro Ecclesia et Pontifice* (Of the Church and the Pope) is outraged that the Duke has not been removed after his attack earlier this year on the Church's official teaching on natural family planning. Last week the Pope reiterated that the natural method is the only acceptable contraception, and even this could be immoral in certain circumstances.

The Catholic Union overwhelmingly supported Miles, who was also backed up by the Cardinal. Miles, henceforth, grew considerably in stature in the eyes of his fellow English Catholics.

8

A Voice in the Lords

As part of his role as 'England's leading Catholic layman' Miles's work in the House of Lords naturally played a major part.

He always favoured – and campaigned for – the elevation to the House of Lords of some suitable spokesmen from the world of institutional religion, a top figure from the British Muslim community, a representative of the Free Churches and the clerical leader of Roman Catholics, Cardinal Hume. The only such person in the Lords in his day (apart, of course, from certain Anglican bishops) was the Chief Rabbi, Lord Jacobovits, whom he knew and admired, and with whom he collaborated more than once on various matters of mutual concern.

Unfortunately, Basil Hume, whom Miles tackled frequently on the issue, remained steadfast in his opposition to the idea. He pointed out that, as far as he was personally concerned, Catholic canon law specifically prohibited the participation of an ordained priest in politics. Miles argued in reply that the Upper House of Britain's Parliament dealt with many matters other than politics. He also pointed out that this canonical ruling was often ignored. Above all, he maintained that views of such leaders would find their ideal audience in the House of Lords, and that their presence there could be of great service to their respective communities on ethical and other matters, and to the nation as a whole. Most Catholics who considered the matter appeared to agree and were disappointed that the Cardinal could not be budged from this particular stance.

Miles never wavered in loyalty to Basil Hume, but he privately very much regretted the Cardinal's refusal to consider sitting in the Lords, which could so easily have been arranged. His regret took on an extra dimension when, from time to time, some Church decision was made from Westminster without any consultation with 'the Laity'. Miles felt it could have been profitably discussed with some such body as the Catholic Union of Great Britain, of which he was president for so many years.

Miles had another reason for hoping that his friend the Cardinal would accept an invitation from the Government to sit in the Lords. He could be excused for pondering – no doubt wistfully – how much it would lessen his own burden of being expected to be the Roman Catholic 'spokesman' in the Lords. As it was, he carried out this duty without complaining; and with considerable skill and success.

It entailed a heavy load of homework, often concerned with complicated technical matters involving medical ethics. From time to time Miles mentions in his diary meetings at the House of Lords or elsewhere with certain people who advised him on the Catholic view about embryos and similar subjects. The chief ones were Phyllis Bowman of SPUC (Society for the Protection of Unborn Children) and Professor Jack Scarisbrick of LIFE. In his entry for 1 December 1989 he notices regretfully that there was a terrible squabble going on between them.

The importance of Miles's conscientious and effective discharge of this duty cannot be overestimated. It must be taken into consideration, moreover, side by side with the quite inaccurate popular image that he emerged as a 'Catholic rebel' after 1984, caused and kept alive by constant allusion in the media to the contraception incident.

The truth was quite the contrary. We have only to consider his attitude to the controversial questions of general morality in the course of his public life. The best guide to this is the record of his speeches in the House of Lords. He spoke forcefully and clearly on all matters of Catholic concern, no matter how controversial or how difficult to explain or defend to a non-Roman Catholic and/or, relatively speaking, indifferent audience. It was a daunting and complicated task, often entailing the mastering of quite complex briefs on unfamiliar (because highly technical) subjects. These included such matters as embryo research, in-vitro fertilisation, rights of the unborn, and many other questions concerning aspects of medical ethics

I have before me as I write a list of all speeches and their subject matter (as extracted from Hansard) made by Miles in the House of Lords between 1971 and 1992. It provides an impressive and extremely interesting résumé of his increasingly active participation in the life of the Upper House. (After 1992 he encouraged other Catholic peers to intervene more often.)

He first sat in Parliament as Lord Beaumont, after the death of his mother on 28 October 1971 and continued to speak there under this title until becoming Duke of Norfolk in 1975.

His participation in the business of the House of Lords was comparatively sparing during the time he sat as Lord Beaumont. Rightly or wrongly he set little store by his abilities as a public speaker. Apart from this, he was still working in the City.

After reaching the prescribed age for retirement from full time employment at Fleming's, i.e. in 1980, he stepped up his Parliamentary work with growing confidence. It was a question of re-tuning his naturally articulate character for a different sort of use. This, combined with his natural and candid, as well as obviously sincere, style of speaking ensured a contribution to the Lords' proceedings which became increasingly effective. It was perhaps his lack of artifice or showmanship that endeared him to the House.

He first sat in Parliament as Duke of Norfolk on 17 April 1975, but did not make any speeches as such until 1976. It is significant that apart from his remarks on Statement of the Defence Estimates (29.4.76), his other four speeches were on: The Incurable Patients' Bill (12.2.76); Obscenity and the Law (24.3.76); Sex and Education of Children (14.1.76); and The Family in Britain Today (16.6.76). This list typifies the sort of subjects on which Miles felt he should intervene in debates.

He was occasionally kind enough to ask me to lunch at the House of Lords and to stay on for some part of the debate afterwards. I heard him speak on several occasions and was invariably impressed. I was also amused to notice another, and quite different, way in which Miles imparted his views to his fellow peers. He was somewhat restless if not impatient by nature and did not take kindly to sitting for lengthy periods listening to the sometimes rather drawn-out orations of their Lordships. Quite frequently he would slip out of his seat and follow some peer out to another part of the building. There he would buttonhole him or her and launch into animated conversation. Other members of the House confirmed this habit of his and told me of the earnest discussions they had had with Miles, almost always at his instigation, in one of the corridors, or in the writing or smoking room, or wherever was convenient. Quite often even, oblivious to interested spectators, Miles would stand at the very door of the debating chamber to hammer home some last-minute point regarding the debate in progress. His remarks were invariably accompanied by much jabbing of his right forefinger, often resulting in vigorous pokes into his companion's shoulder or lapel. Whether or not you agreed with what he was saying, Miles had an arresting way of compelling attention by his animated enthusiasm for the point he was making. Viewing this spectacle from a distance could be rather like watching a woodpecker.

It would be impossible to summarise all of Miles's interventions in the House of Lords, just as it is impossible to give an exact estimate of how many of these there were. A lot depends on whether you include every single intervention, however short. However, as far as I have been able to see from my list taken from Hansard, Miles made over a hundred main speeches between 1981 and 1999, which is a respectable record for a back-bench peer, a position Miles was always determined to maintain.

His mastery of the material needed for use in his speeches on such matters as embryo research, rights of unborn children, and similar topics was very impressive. Often he had to produce vigorous arguments in favour of some distinctly 'unpopular' cause, concerning for example, the sanctity at every stage of human life. I admired him for his valiant efforts in this direction, never diverting an iota from strictly orthodox Catholic teaching. Inevitably, in circumstances such as these, he was not always successful. But I remember one case in which he made a particular mark.

It was on 14 December 1989. The debate was on a private member's bill to reduce the normal legal upper limits for abortion from 28 to 24 weeks. It was typical of Miles that he did not confine his arguments to narrow and purely moralistic ones. In fact he took this particular opportunity to make some general remarks about Catholic belief which were widely publicised at the time and stayed in people's memories for some time afterwards.

Before coming to particular points regarding the morality of the legislation being proposed, Miles dismissed as 'nonsense' the accusation that he was trying to force his religious views on everyone else. He went on to say: 'Thank God the Spanish Inquisition was wound up three centuries ago. Any religious domination is appalling. I do not believe everything the Roman Catholic Church says, though I think on the whole it has the best ideas.'

The last sentence was probably one of the most succinct and effective statements Miles ever made, at least in public, about the nature of his Catholic belief.

His attempt to kill the Abortion Bill under discussion did not succeed. His amendment however, was only defeated by 68 votes to 41, which was very far from being a crushing defeat.

On 6 February 1990 he supported the fears of a number of other peers that a proposed Human Fertilisation and Embryology Bill would permit unlicensed experiments on living, out-of-the-womb embryos for the first thirty hours of their existence. Miles's contribution to the debate – his side lost overwhelmingly – contained a typical plea for honesty and absence of double-talk. It should be said 'in plain English that we want no experiments from fertilisation onwards. We want an embryo defined from the beginning of fertilisation.'

Some idea of the frustration in supporting unpopular causes such as these can be obtained by considering the subject matter of what turned out to be surprisingly lively debate on 25 July 1991. Miles, supported by Baroness Hooper, was pressing Her Majesty's Government on whether it was content to license a drug called Mifeopristone for abortion, bearing in mind that it was otherwise only licensed in France. Such licensing depended on the Medicines Act of 1968 and was subject to the Abortion Act of 1967. The fear now was that insufficient time was being allowed for testing before a licence was granted.

Miles and Lady Hooper at least achieved a delay. Both were doughty fighters, but campaigners such as these must have been discouraged by the paucity of interested headlines despite so much laborious work behind the scenes. One of Miles's great qualities was that he never gave up.

It is cheering to be able to report one triumph in the House of Lords associated with Miles. It occurred on 13 March 1980 and was headlined by the *Daily Telegraph* as a 'Rout for Tories by Lords'. It was not, admittedly, on a matter of shattering international or even national importance. But it was an important milestone in its own way. It contained, moreover, an element of justice and humanitarian concern which particularly whetted Miles's appetite for a tussle.

What, in brief, happened was that as the result of a sturdy combined stand by Miles and Lord Butler of Saffron Walden, a Government-sponsored scheme to enable councils to charge for school transport was rejected by a majority of 104. It was very much part of Miles's abiding interest in educational matters, Catholic and other.

The Government that was defeated on this occasion, incidentally, was headed by none other than Margaret Thatcher. The huge vote against the Government secured banner headlines. I remember the occasion well and was told by several people at the time that Margaret was not best pleased!

All in all Miles can be said to have kept the Catholic flag flying for thirty years in the Lords in a way that was not just adequate but outstanding. His good-natured sincerity and lack of fanaticism – combined with an impressive grasp of his facts – won him respect in every corner of the House. It must be remembered, moreover, that Miles, a scrupulous and regular attendee of the House, took a vigorous part in its business at every level. But it was often a hard and thankless task, involving much committee work and study at home.

PART FOUR

'Sufficiently Senior'

I

Through the Looking Glass

For a continuous period of nearly sixty years Miles kept a diary which faithfully recorded daily events but seldom made what could be called 'in-depth' comments on his activities. His basic system was to keep a day-to-day record consisting of short entries, later dictating the whole to a secretary. For many years, during the later phase of his life, this was a lady called Eileen Wallace, of whom Miles spoke most warmly. As an 'amanuensis' she was ideal and Miles relied on her totally.

A brief explanation is meanwhile required of the title of this part of the book, 'Sufficiently Senior.' It comes from an expression used by Miles himself in his diary to describe that period in his later life when he was 'sufficiently senior' not to have automatically to sit next to the Queen – or ranking member of the royal family – at official functions. The object of this intentional break in protocol was to enable more junior members of the household to sit in the place of honour.

Anne kindly entrusted me with the carefully typed transcripts of all the diaries. It was tempting to make fairly liberal use of them, quoting them quite fully. For the most part, however, they referred to the relatively humdrum events of daily life, amounting to little more than a glorified appointment book. I have therefore confined myself, up to now, to quoting from them only when some snippet catches Miles's character.

In the following pages, however, I have made a major departure from this general principle. The reason for this is that, from time to time, especially later on, Miles himself made exceptions to his basic pattern of diary-keeping. If some important topic came up, connected with, say, the Church or his public duties, Miles, instead of inserting the usual one-line reference in his diary, would expand on it at some length, sometimes several typed pages. I have thus selected a few of the more characteristic or trenchant passages, giving his views on some issues he considered important. They also have the value of giving a first-hand example of Miles's distinctive style and way of thinking.

13 January 1992 The new Black Rod was installed, Admiral Sir Richard Thomas, KCB, OBE. He and his wife have a flat in the Houses of Parliament and they also, curiously, must be something to do with Black Rod's garden which is where we are now parking our cars on the upstream side of the House of Lords, quite close to the Memorial to the Burghers of Calais by Rodin. He runs, under the Lord Great Chamberlain, the supervision of the House of Lords and other parts of the Houses of Parliament, except the House of Commons, which took over their parts of the Palace of Westminster some time earlier this century. He is of course a vital friend to me and we lay on together, for instance, the annual Opening of Parliament. When I die, Eddie must be careful to ensure that Black Rod and the Lord Great Chamberlain are under him, and I emphasised this by changing my position at the Opening ceremony to walking backwards in front of The Queen, not in front of The Duke of Edinburgh.

When Bernard died, Hugh Cholmondeley could not have been more helpful to me but he, amazingly, made me agree that he should walk in front of The Queen to which I readily agreed but now I have reasserted the Earl Marshal's position. In all these Orders of Precedence the Earl Marshal, if a Duke, is superior to the Lord Great Chamberlain, who is only a Marquess and if he had been a Duke, the Earl Marshal would be junior to him. I might also add that the Lord Great Chamberlain dates from Henry III's reign and some time there must have been a row, because all the organisation of the Palace parties and the inside of the Palaces is now done by the Lord Chamberlain and the only place where the Lord Great Chamberlain has authority is in the Houses of Parliament.

This digression also gives me a chance to let Eddie know that when I die he will be wise to be humble at first, as I know he will, in Parliament, and take advice from the many young peers he knows. They will tell him how one can sit on the steps of the Throne; and the wisdom of choosing an area in the back benches always to be found; and the wise rules of procedure for speaking. I am sure I was right to sit as a Conservative, whereas Bernard sat on the Cross Benches, but his father sat at first with the Liberals and then with the Tories.

Eddie will find, as head of the Catholic Union and the inevitable leader of the Catholic peers, he will have to take on religious, ethical and moral problems, and there are many inter-house parliamentary societies such as the All-Party Pro-Life Group of which Ann Winterton MP is now the Chairman. I maintain it was very silly of Cardinal Hume not to accept a life peerage which Margaret Thatcher offered him two or three years ago when she also offered one to the head Jewish pastor, Jacobovits, who accepted. Cardinal Basil never told me, as President of the Catholic Union, he had refused, but one has little contact with the hierarchy, which I greatly regret, and I learned of this from Lord Shackleton, who was the Liberal peer on some committee where all parties are represented to vet new peerages, which was set up at the time when Lloyd George was selling peerages to anyone who gave £20,000 to the Liberal Party.

I got to know Chief Rabbi myself slightly during my years as Treasurer of the Council of Christians and Jews. His description of his meetings with Miles was 'exhilarating,' while Miles, for his part, greatly liked and admired the Chief Rabbi. Miles once told me that it was only since getting to know Jacobovits that he realised that the accusations against the Church concerning its nineteen centuries of fostering a dangerous form of anti-Semitism were not so wide of the mark after all.

17 March 1993 I saw Cardinal Basil at 11.45 ... I had not seen him for a personal discussion for two or three years and I mentioned how disappointed I was that he had not taken up the seat offered him in the House of Lords as a life peer by Margaret Thatcher, about which he had never told me, which I think he should have done. He then told me that he had also been offered to be a life peer by Callaghan. I mentioned that his presence would have been invaluable in the Abortion Debates and that now, having lost our points, there are abortions of about 600 or 800 a day, which is roughly speaking a battalion strength and utterly awful. It is a customary method of birth control. I also mentioned that I hoped the rest of the Hierarchy will come out into the open and not give the appearance of enjoying living in a sort of sacred ghetto, believing they were so much more holy than the Anglican and the other faiths. Cardinal Basil said one of the reasons he had declined being made a life peer was he felt the Catholic Bishops should not be treated as second class spiritual leaders and that, say, five or so of them should be made Lords Spiritual like the twenty-six Anglican Bishops. I pointed out this would really raise the question of House of Lords reform which was a moot point, always lying in the background.

Subsequently, as will be seen in my files, Lord Renton approached me about Basil becoming a life peer, and I discovered it was tied up with the general fear that the Anglican Church might become disestablished and that the presence of Cardinal Basil as a life peer might help to defer it.

I must emphasise that the presence of Catholic Bishops would relieve the pressure on the Catholic peers in such subjects as education where, at the moment, the Anglican point of view is being strongly expressed by the Bishop of Guildford, who is an expert and was once the Archbishop of Canterbury's Private Secretary.

18 March 1993 I have been attending Parliament a lot and in principle two major bills are going through: one, on further trade union reform, which originated with Margaret Thatcher and is still much needed, for they are still much too powerful and act in restraint of trade, and of course are the paymasters of the Labour Party which, later, the Labour Leader, Smith, is about to curb and so split the Labour Party. The second bill is the Housing and Leasehold Reform Act which, again, is a legacy of Margaret Thatcher and seeks to enable all leaseholders to buy their tenancies. I am not yet clear as to the merits of this, and much appreciate that it would be the end of the big leasehold estates, such as that of the Duke of Westminster and many other charitable property holdings. I have only once voted for the Government, and kept away when I realised that it would benefit me in that I might be able to buy the leasehold of 61 Clabon Mews.

5 March 1996 There was a Grenadier dinner at the Royal Hospital to celebrate the retirement on reaching 70, or some such age, of General Sir David Fraser, having been a Regimental Trustee for many years.

The following extracts are included as examples – virtually at random – of the hundreds, indeed thousands, of day-to-day comments made by Miles in the course of his sixty or so years of diary-keeping.

7 March 1996 I gave Willie Nagel[1] and Mariegold and Mirabel[2] lunch in the House of Lords. That evening Anne and I had dinner with Albert and Monique Roux, who runs Le Gavroche restaurant. He is charming and a superb cook.

8 March 1996 I and Brigadier Michael Biggs and others were filmed for the KAR records at Sandhurst. I have a copy of the resulting video tape.

10 March 1996 I attended Evensong at St George's, Windsor when the Garter Banner belonging to Lavinia (Norfolk) was laid up.

The next, quite long, extract gives a good idea of Miles's views on the procedure and significance of the House of Lords, and includes his recurring disappointment that Cardinal Hume persisted in his refusal to accept a peerage.

15 October 1996 The House of Lords returned from its long summer holiday and as readers of this diary well know, I go there whenever I can and take part, but I am always very concerned that one cannot speak without having prepared oneself, for it is indeed an assembly of experts. It is of course absurd that Cardinal Hume will not attend and an interesting situation is developing. Namely, if there is a House of Lords reform at the General Election by Blair on 1 May and he seeks to abolish the voting by the hereditary peers, the Anglican Bishops will find themselves also excluded and therefore they are very interested in buttressing the keeping of their seats by having Catholic Bishops also given seats and, in addition, Jews and Mohammedans. I am in fact dictating this on 30 April 1997.

Most of us hereditary peers feel we do a good revisionary job as a second chamber and not enough people realise that on the one

1 Long-time Jewish friend and generous contributor to Anne's charity.
2 Youngest sister.

hand the Tory Party is always well represented by the 'Back-woodsmen', but on the other hand the Labour Party is well repre-sented by the Salisbury Convention which was arranged when Attlee threatened to abolish the House of Lords in 1945 and 'Bobbety' Salisbury agreed that anything in a Labour manifesto on which the Labour Party won the election must be passed in principle, although of course it could be revised and sharpened up. It would be an absurdity for the present House of Lords to contain only life peers who are Prime Ministers' nominations and we must go for a fully elected chamber. I have often thought a simple solu-tion would be to copy Thomas Jefferson's and Hamilton's Senate in the United States, where they had two senators per state, elected for six years. If we grouped our counties into the 60 constituen-cies that now elect European Parliamentary MPs, that would make a House of − 2 per constituency − of 120. But this would mean a house with powers over money bills and everything, which would of course then become a great rival to the Commons.

So many bills at the moment start in the Commons with, say, 50 clauses, but they filibuster away and only 10 are done, and the other 40 clauses are all debated in detail in the Lords, with the briefs being sent up. There is no filibustering in the Lords − if it starts any peer can move that 'the Noble Lord be no longer heard this day' and this is voted on and that stops him filibustering. Revising this draft today, on 16 May, I can add that Lord Cran-borne, who is the Leader of the Conservatives in the House of Lords, told me on 14 May at the Opening of Parliament that his plan is for the Commons to have a Select Committee on the future of the House of Lords because they are elected representatives of the people and they should decide. There are so many plans being discussed by individual peers, such as the hereditary peers elect-ing, say, 50 or 100 of their number to sit in Parliament after elec-tion. But I really doubt whether this is likely in the modern democratic political set-up.

The next extract may seem surprising. In its own rather quaint way, you may think that it gives an interesting insight into a more hidden part of Miles's character, namely his imaginative thoughtfulness about out-of-the-way topics, and the human interest involved therein. It also displays, if only indirectly, his abiding love for anything to do with Carlton. In another sense it can perhaps be looked at as an intriguing essay on social history.

At some date, probably in the 18th century, the ancestor of Carlton built a bank to stop his immediate park and farm land flooding. The bank started at the Templehurst Road and went south, being the boundary of the small lake, and then the present cricket field and on along the field being farmed by Eddell, to the Snaith side of the big lake and, eastwards, between the 20-acre field and Festival Folly Wood to Baffin Hill Wood, where it petered out, since Baffin Hill is a small hill. It then was re-created to go north through Long Wood and Three-Pigeon Wood and Kennel Wood, where, again, it peters out because there is a small hill, on which the present Keeper's Cottage is built. The area inside this bank would clearly be sheltered from the perennial floods. Incidentally, there was a windmill to grind the corn just north of the present Keeper's Cottage, which I have never seen because it was dismantled before my time.

2 Presumably the windmill was dismantled when coal came into use to create steam power in the 1850s and, up to the 2nd World War, every factory had its own little steam engine to create power to turn its machinery. Such was the case of the Clog Mills at Snaith, but towns like Selby and Pontefract had many such little steam power plants. However, after the 2nd World War all these steam engines were replaced by electricity, and I can remember the creation of the big electrical power stations such as Ferrybridge just before the war, with their power lines stretching across the countryside. From the top of the tower at Carlton Towers one can see now Ferrybridge power station, Eggborough, Barnby Dun which is now being dismantled, and Drax which is a double power station, the largest in Europe. All of them are steam powered, using the coal of the Yorkshire coalfield. Interestingly, the Hull and Barnsley railway line was built to unload wooden pit props at Hull, being landed from Scandinavia and transported to Barnsley, and the reverse train carried coal which was exported from Barnsley to Hull and then shipped round the world. This railway line is at present used from the Barnsley area to Drax

where it terminates and the onward line to Hull has been pulled up. I can remember the one passenger train per day which every line had to run running through Carlton Station and these trains were called the Parliamentary and the charge was a penny a mile. Another line was the line from Lancashire passing through Snaith to Goole as part of the Lancashire/Yorkshire railway which had wonderful purple engines. There were something like 70 railway companies, some of which were going broke and so they were consolidated around 1920 into the four big companies: the LNER, the LMS, the Southern and the Great Western.

3 It must have been remarkable to have lived in the 1840s when the railways started passenger transport so that people could travel to London and elsewhere, whereas before only the rich people could very expensively afford to go by coach. It is of course well-known that the Duke of Bridgewater built the English canal system in the 1820s and 30s but the railways soon came and so the canals were never properly used. My grandmother used to box her horses at Snaith to go hunting, say, near Knottingley with the Badsworth Hunt when the railway company would put on a special train for the Hunt. Grannie also used to ride bicycles even as far as Scarborough, 60 miles away, when they came in, in the 1880s, and apparently there were many house parties when the guests brought their bicycles.

4 I should also mention how, with our large walled garden, we had great fruit and vegetable production but, when winter came, few vegetables were preserved, apart from potatoes in large piles on each farm and similarly turnips for the cattle; and we also had eggs put in water glass, which sealed the shells so they lasted till the spring. And then tinning of vegetables and fruit started, to preserve them, but these all tasted so different from the fresh fruit and, finally, as electricity became established the fridge took over and, nowadays, one has fresh everything because it is frozen. At Carlton we did have an ice pit near the old green door entrance to the village (10 yards from the Stapleton Lodge House) in the woods, where clearly blocks of ice from the floods in the Templehurst Road were hauled up and stored, packed with leaves which, amazingly, preserved the ice.

5 We had, which was quite rare, an electric light plant at the

Towers of 100 volts, built in 1914, and it operated on gas produced from anthracite coal. Alas, this wonderful engine with a 6-foot flywheel was sold and destroyed when we went on the electricity power line, which came to Carlton just before the war. I can well remember the efforts made by the Yorkshire Electricity Power Company to get enough people in the village to agree to have electric light so that a sub-line from Snaith would pay. For instance Fr Duane, the Parish Priest, openly said we must have it in the Catholic Church from the pulpit.

The next extract is a reiteration of Miles's views on lay relations with the Catholic hierarchy.

8 April 1997 I lunched with Mariegold in her flat and attended the Low Week Cardinal Basil cocktail party where I was deliberately rude to Bishop David Konstant and Vincent Nichols for having failed to consult the Catholic Union when they wrote their pamphlet called The Common Good. As I said in a letter to Cardinal Basil, it is disgraceful how the Catholic Hierarchy treat the Laity as peasants.

I now refer to a diary entry by Miles of a slightly different nature, but illustrating, which I think, is important, his well-informed interest in Catholic affairs, including those not generally known. I add, with apologies, some comment of my own having been indirectly involved in the matter mentioned.

In his diary entry for 1 May 1987, Miles wrote: 'About this time I have noted that the *Catholic Herald* tried to buy the *Universe* for £1.35 million but the Bishops bought it for £1.25 million.'

For the purposes of the transaction in question, the Bishops set up a company called Gabriel Communications to be, in their name, the nominal purchasers of *The Universe* newspaper. Our bid – that is on behalf of *The Catholic Herald* – was presumably never put to the shareholders of *The Universe*, even though it was substantially higher than that of the Bishops. In this case the eventual purchase was irregular and possibly illegal.

To his diary reference to the affair Miles added the further comment: 'Rumour has it that the very right-wing group Opus Dei was trying to buy *The Universe* and the Catholic bishops had to forestall them.'

Miles, in other words, had stumbled on some interesting facts and it was certainly true that the hierarchy did not want to see this widely circulating Catholic newspaper falling into what Miles described as 'crypto-fascist' hands. For quite different reasons, the Bishops were also reluctant for the new owners to be the *Catholic Herald*. The same paper (*The Universe*) is known (at the time of writing) once more to be up for sale. Perhaps we (the *Catholic Herald*) will finally buy it after all.

The next and final diary extract finds Miles expressing himself forcefully about the undeserved ill-fortune that befell his old friend Father Michael Hollings, who was indeed a very remarkable man.

27 October 1999 Michael Hollings came to stay the weekend at Bacres. Some weeks ago an article appeared in *The News of the World* by a certain John … who is a Sikh. Michael Hollings, when he was a parish priest at Southall, which has many Sikhs around, took in down-and-outs and let them sleep on sofas and in sleeping bags in the Presbytery, and this John told *The News of the World* that Michael Hollings had fumbled him and hinted it was a sexual matter. Most unfortunately Clifford Longley referred *to all* of this in his weekly article in the *Telegraph* and then I rang up *The Tablet* and told John Wilkins, the Editor, he must surely not think of reporting this in *The Tablet*; but John said he had already written of it because the Church's policy now was to cover up nothing. I was furious but failed to dissuade him from publishing it. The result of this publicity is that Michael Hollings has been officially suspended by the Cardinal, and the case of 25 years ago is being investigated by the diocese. Most disgracefully this case has dragged on with Michael Hollings not being allowed to perform in his parish even though the parish has vociferously demanded he should return. And, later, in December, the Cardinal was advised that there would be no further investigation by the Canon Lawyers, but the matter was disgracefully put in the hands of the Social Services and Michael Hollings was told the Archdiocese would pay for a solicitor. This case of Michael Hollings being forbidden to visit his parish at St Mary of the Angels dragged on until Sunday, 18 February, when Cardinal Hume said two Masses in the Church and announced that Michael Hollings would be reinstated. There was universal clapping at this news. Cardinal

Basil also announced that Michael Hollings would be allowed to stay there as Parish Priest until death, which is a considerable pat on the back, for most priests have to retire at 75 and he is something like 74 now.

I end this chapter by offering a sample of a slightly different kind of what Miles himself wrote. He had been asked to give the after-dinner speech to the New York members of the Pilgrims' Society, attracting people with Anglo-American connections or interests. As far as I remember I had originally proposed Miles's membership to the Pilgrims (in Great Britain) and he thereafter became a distinguished and valuable participant.

The subject of Miles's speech was to be 'The Current Communist Threat to Christendom', but Miles wrote a preliminary draft which while being quite different from the speech he delivered, contained a lot of information about himself and his family. This is why I have reproduced it here rather than the actual, finished speech. This draft was sent, on 20 February 1979, to two people for their opinion. These were Charles de Salis, husband of Anne's sister Carolyn, and Sir Paul Wright, a distinguished retired ambassador.

THE CURRENT THREAT TO CHRISTENDOM (DRAFT)

1 *Introduction* Great honour to be invited to speak at the Pilgrims' dinner. I can humbly claim I am no stranger here since I spent two years as a Major in the British Army in the Pentagon from 1947 to 1949 and have visited America many times and touched down in over 40 of your States.

Furthermore, my children can say Granny comes from Texas.

2 *Norfolk Family History* Some of you may have read of the immense wealth of the Duke of Westminster who owns half of Mayfair and indeed it was said in Lloyd George's time that to maintain a Dukedom cost about as much as a new battleship, but I can assure you my life has been very little changed by my cousin, Bernard Norfolk, having died four years ago. Indeed the other day I picked up the telephone and answered that I was the Duke of Norfolk and a voice came back saying 'What's that, a pub?'

The family history is so colourful that you might consider the start to be shocking pink for I fear there is little doubt that the first

Howard Duke of Norfolk was probably implicated with Richard III in the disappearance of the two Princes in the Tower in 1483.

In a remarkable way we remained true to the Catholic Faith and indeed from our point of view the Reformation was a load of rubbish because the other County families got the land, such as the Cecils, and we lost our heads. Two of my ancestors were beheaded on Tower Hill, the Poet Earl and his son, the 4th Duke, who was accused of plotting to marry Mary Queen of Scots. His son Philip died in the Tower because he refused to give up his Faith and is now a canonised Saint; and yet another ancestor, the 3rd Duke, was condemned to be beheaded but with a bit of Howard luck Henry VIII died the night before and so he was reprieved.

Saint Philip's son, Thomas, the Collecting Earl, was the forerunner of patrons of the arts. He got his hooks on over 700 pictures and took Inigo Jones to Italy where he became enthused with the Renaissance and Palladio. The building of the Queen's House at Greenwich by Inigo Jones was the forerunner of the Palladian architecture which you so happily call the Colonial style. The Collecting Earl also collected the Arundel Marbles and a magnificent library but the 6th Duke couldn't have cared less so they were all given away to the Ashmolean Museum and the Royal Society.

The 11th Duke was a great friend of the Prince Regent and could drink him and others under the table without difficulty. He was a gross and famous figure whom the footmen liked to get drunk so they could get him washed. I might mention I am not descended from him but many people are, and we keep on having enquiries which always go back to him.

3 *English History* There is no need to remind an audience such as you how our history is unique in Western Europe owing to our island fastness. Unlike Continental countries our Queen can trace her descent back to Cedric of the Wessex dynasty in the 6th century and we have had no revolution since 1660 so that we evolve at a slow pace and indeed at the moment are in the throes of a silent but violent clash of political forces which I have no doubt we will solve in our own way without bloodshed; and I personally believe if the night is a little dark the dawn is at hand.

4 *Religious History* All my Howard ancestors are Catholics except for the Collecting Earl, but of course there are many cousins in our vast clan who are members of the Church of England. Nevertheless the family are thought of as being the bastion of the Old Faith. I have said I am descended from Saint Philip Howard and it happens that my wife is directly descended from Sir Thomas More, and let me give you the happy news of how the English Christians are basking now in the friendship of ecumenism. We had Catholic emancipation in 1829 and other small disabilities were gradually repealed and now we are about to have a Catholic Lord Chancellor.[3] Cardinal Hume addressed the Synod of the Church of England standing between the Archbishops of York and Canterbury. Prince Charles read the lesson at Westminster Cathedral and the Queen is coming to the Flower Festival there this summer. I am really over here to endow the building and in particular the Westminster Choir School after the immensely successful appeal in England to raise £1 million to which the Queen subscribed.

Last year was the year of the three Popes and, having had an audience with the present Pope, I look forward to immense progress in understanding and Christian charity throughout the world.

5 This address must not be a platitudinous history of the past. Let me ask you to consider what it is that makes, as you so neatly say, us all tick. The world has clearly now polarised between two conflicting philosophies, the Communist and those who believe in God; to Christianity I would add other religions such as Jews and Mohammedans who after all both believe in the same God the Father as we do.

6 *Communism* There are many variations of communism, the Russian variation which is really a cloak for Russian imperialism; there is Oriental communism in China and Vietnam; there is Eurocommunism in Italy and France, but they all have one characteristic, that they depend on the false tenets of the Marx-Englian materialism that a perfect political morality would evolve and the

---

3 It was thought, at this time, that Lord Rawlinson would be the next Lord Chancellor, but this never happened – chiefly because Lord Hailsham was reluctant to give up his place on the Woolsack.

need for state supervision would wither away. But this has never happened and communism only survives under the beastly tyranny of the Politburo and Red Army or its equivalent.

7 *Christianity* Let us contrast this communist view of man as self-ish and slothful, needing oppression, with the Christian recognition of human nature as being a union of body and spirit with God as the ultimate purpose of life. Unlike an animal, man can distinguish good from evil and must have the right to choose for himself and his family. Self-denial and charity are meaningless without a belief in God, so the communist states cannot inspire man to lead a devoted life.

8 *Conclusion* And surely we can allow ourselves a little joy when we reflect that the tide is beginning to turn and the youth of the world is now hungering not for communism but for freedom under the law and it has begun to appreciate, particularly in China, the booming returns that a capitalist economy yields in contrast to the dead drabness of socialism.

2
'Retirement'

I have put the title to this penultimate chapter in quotation marks for a special reason, namely that the evening of Miles's life was strikingly different from that of most men of his age. He virtually never actually retired but rather, as attested by his full diary entries until his very last months, his days were crowded with energetic and enthusiastic activity. Always reluctant to say 'no' to a challenge or an invitation, chiefly because of a desire not to disappoint, he often, as time went on, had to be persuaded by Anne or his doctor to curb his enthusiasm and restless urge to be ever on-the-move.

I have seldom, if ever, known anyone other than Miles who so perfectly embodied the maxim *mens sane in corpore sano*. His perceptive mind, which never became clouded, complemented a healthy physique that owed much to a well-ordered and regular life-style, sensible diet and to the fact that he was tough and wiry and never put on weight with age. He maintained his lean and rather slight figure to the end, despite concern for his health from time to time. From about the Seventies onwards, that is for nearly the last twenty years of his life, he relied on a pacemaker to keep his heart stable, and on the able counselling of a succession of excellent doctors whom he trusted and obeyed, including Howard Swanton of the Middlesex Hospital.

Most of his sojourns in hospital were occasioned by the need for – usually orthopaedic – surgery. In early 1983, as I happen to remember, we were in rooms near to each other in Sister Agnes's – the King Edward VII Hospital in Beaumont Street. He was undergoing traction for a leg injury while I was having a hip replacement. The doctor for both of us was Ronald Sweetnam (whom Miles could never get out of the habit of calling 'Sweetman'), and the Chairman of Sister Agnes's at the time, whom we both knew, was Sir Mark Baring.[1] His visits often turned into social occasions, with Miles

1 Mark Baring's widow Vita later married Miles's brother Michael.

bringing a 'life-and-soul-of-the-party' atmosphere to the hospital. All of this was greatly assisted by the kindness of the Matron who made sure that if we were ever brought such welcome gifts by visiting friends as half-bottles of champagne, these were duly kept in the fridge with appropriate glasses supplied as needed.

One evening Cardinal Hume was kind enough to come and visit me and I said 'Oh, I expect you know, Father Basil, that's Miles's room is down the passage. Shall we go and see him?'

'Definitely not,' replied the Cardinal with a twinkle in his eye. 'I've just come from there and we'd better not go back. He'll only start banging on again about myself and the House of Lords or some such topic!'

Miles's unabated activity throughout his twilight – but never darkened – years continued to be a mixture of scrupulous attention to his public duties, Catholic and charity work, a varied social life, and enthusiastic hobbies. The mixture in his case, moreover, was balanced and sensible as he belonged to numerous clubs and societies, often involving – to him, sometimes rather tedious – formal dinners. He disliked dressing up, particularly in a white tie, and preferred the more relaxed atmosphere of regimental or college reunions or similar occasions.

We were both members, for example, of the Pitt Club which organised interesting and enjoyable dinners twice a year in London. The summer dinners were invariably held at the hall of some Livery company and Miles always stuck to his habit, after eating and drinking frugally, of leaving in time to be home by about eleven or soon after. Soon after ten, if I happened to catch his eye, he would say 'Now look here, isn't it about time for us to walk home?' Yes – I literally mean *walk*. Even for quite long distances, Miles would rarely if ever accept a lift or take a taxi. Instead he would dive down to the cloakroom to retrieve his rather shabby cap, which he always wore even with a dinner jacket, and he would boldly stride off through the deserted City streets. He never carried a walking stick but would keep up the brisk pace all the way home to Chelsea. I walked a lot myself in those days – alas no longer – but must confess that my slight advantage in years over Miles was little help in keeping up with his athletic military strides. He would arrive home in no way out of breath; no wonder he kept fit for so long.

When, much later, he did begin showing signs of slowing up, he managed to postpone for as long as possible any serious deterioration. There were two serious scares in the year 2001, indicating that the end might be nigh. On each occasion he kept the Reaper at bay. His survival seemed nothing short of miraculous. Anne, in talking to a friend, said she could only account for it by the fact that the Good Lord must be dreading the chaos he might cause when he got to heaven and so was postponing that moment for as long as possible. When Miles finally met his Creator, I can't help feeling that his first words were 'Now look here ...' followed by a spirited dissertation on some pressing problem.

Apart from work and family affairs, the latter always being a top priority, Miles pursued his various hobbies with characteristic energy. These often included strenuous manual labour – such as chopping down trees in which he involved his, often not entirely voluntary, house-guests. Picture-framing was probably his favourite avocation, and at this he became something of an expert. He framed all Anne's increasingly attractive and skilful paintings which was a tremendous help to her and doubtless, if indirectly, increased the resulting sums which they raised for the Hospices. He spent many happy hours over this in the cluttered workroom at Bacres when he was not reading or writing in his library, which contained an impressively eclectic collection of books and records.

His voracious reading habits followed him everywhere he went. My wife and I joined him and Anne on several holidays, for example to Martinique, Grenada, Dominica, Madeira and St Kitts, where Rawlins Plantation was a felicitous discovery of the Norfolks. It was there that Miles told me so much about his life during our long after-lunch conversations.

During these holidays Anne would start painting immediately after breakfast, barely stopping even for lunch. She was a prolific producer of painting in her own distinctive style, which got better and better over the years and netted substantial sums for Help the Hospices. Her exhibitions, about every two years, would be enthusiastically attended. In all, including the sale of cards taken from her pictures, she has raised over half a million pounds for hospice care. On holiday, when we all congregated for pre-dinner cocktails, no one deserved her vodkatini as much as Anne after her long hours of painting, usually standing up all day.

Miles always brought with him a plentiful supply of the latest books, constantly, however, breaking off his reading to have a chat or engage some (possibly rather startled) new arrival at the resort in animated conversation. During such holidays, Miles's first preoccupation was to ascertain the whereabouts of the nearest Catholic Church and the times of Masses.

I might add here a corollary to what I have said elsewhere about Miles's views on the Catholic liturgical reforms of relatively recent years. He did not share the mistaken view of some Catholics that the so-called 'traditional' – or 'Latin' – Mass was of genuine antiquity. It had gradually developed during the late Middle Ages, whereas the liturgy that has replaced it in modern times is based on the Eucharistic worship of the earliest Christian centuries. One of the features of this ancient liturgy was the exchanging of a sign of peace.

Our weekly holiday attendances at the most convenient Catholic church, especially in the West Indies, always represented an elaborate and joyous expression of brotherhood and friendship. The venerable liturgical action, though often mistakenly considered modern, dates from the earliest days when Christians were pacifists. 'If we tried that in England,' Miles remarked at lunch one day after Mass, 'everyone would just sit around looking po-faced.' Newcomers at the resort would, within half an hour, find themselves chatting with Miles as if they had know him for years, and he could get away, by sheer charm and piquancy, with sometimes saying outrageous things.

One evening some Americans arrived and Miles asked them to join us for drinks before lunch. The subject, for some reason, of surnames cropped up and Miles said 'Yes, I've had lots of them.' They looked puzzled. 'Well, you see,' explained Miles, 'when I left the Army I was plain Major-General Howard, and no one spoke to me. When I became Lord Beaumont, things picked up. Then came Lord Howard of Glossop, and now that I'm a Duke I'm quite popular.'

'Outdoor hobbies', of course, had always been plentiful, especially – from his youngest days – shooting. His shooting parties were jolly and informal and he was always the most unpompous of hosts, often, if need be, taking a minor part in the proceedings. Marie-Lou de Zulueta, an old friend of Miles, told me that her late husband Philip was once asked to come up and shoot at Carlton. He said he would love to but, as he had recently had a heart attack, could he ask for the services of a loader? When he arrived and they were preparing for the first drive, he mentioned to another guest that no loader seemed to be in the offing.

Miles, overhearing his remark, said 'Oh, it's quite all right, Philip. I'm your loader.'

Not long after this, a film (*A Handful of Dust*) was made at Carlton, and Miles played a walk-on part as a gardener. Invariably wearing rather rough-and-ready country clothes, Miles presumed he was 'tailor-made' for the part. He was quite surprised when the director said: 'If you don't mind, Your Grace, we'll have to dress you up a bit. And, by the way, real gardeners don't bow so low!'

Soon after becoming a duke, he sat down one morning at his desk at Fleming's and was confronted with a rather serious-looking inter-office memo. It turned out to be from his brother-in-law, and fellow director, Jerry Jamieson, and contained the following mock-serious typed message: 'It has come to the attention of the directors that Dukes are normally expected to own grouse moors but that the Duke of Norfolk does not have one. (signed) J. Jamieson.' Underneath was the hand-written note: 'If you get one, I'll come and shoot there (if asked!)'

Miles, taking the hint, forthwith acquired a fine grouse moor called Arkengarthdale in Yorkshire. Many successful shoots were held at 'Arken' – as Miles always called it in his diary –and the moor still flourishes in the care of his son Eddie.

Bill Merton, Chairman of Fleming's at the time, has related how there was once a fire at their offices and everyone was ordered out into the street. When the fire brigade arrived, the Chief Fire Officer shouted out the question 'Who is your Marshal?' A voice (Miles's) answered 'I'm the Earl Marshal. Will that do?'

Miles, while always scrupulously correct as regards his official duties, invariably added a welcome dimension of good-humoured informality to their discharge (without ever distracting from the dignity of the occasion.) My wife and I, for example, were once invited by the Norfolks to attend the opening of Parliament. Anne and the guests occupied a box in the long gallery immediately opposite the stairs at the top of which the Queen would appear just after first entering the Palace of Westminster.

At this stage, all the waiting officials would stand stiffly to attention – with the notable exception of Miles. He would wander about exchanging banter with various people nearby and, on this occasion, came up to where we were sitting. I happened to be just behind the French Ambassador who was sitting in the front row. When Miles wandered over, Anne introduced him. 'His Excellency' was formally attired in morning suit and was obviously impressed by the occasion and surroundings.

'I say, look here,' Miles immediately said on discovering to whom he was talking; 'You see the picture over that door? That's King Henry V. He's the one who saw your lot off at Agincourt!'

Writing this book has brought back many happy memories. It has been a privilege to try and pay tribute, however inadequately, to such a very special person. R.I.P.

PART FIVE
Servant of the State

Epilogue

JOHN MARTIN ROBINSON

When Miles inherited the dukedom he entered with energy and enthusiasm into the new official life which came with it, notably the hereditary role of Earl Marshal of England in charge of state ceremonial. His predecessor, Bernard, had been Earl Marshal for over fifty years and had been responsible for organising two funerals of the Sovereign, the state funeral of Sir Winston Churchill, two Coronations and the Investiture of the Prince of Wales, becoming a well-known public figure in this role in the television age. Miles in his twenty-five years as Earl Marshal had no state funeral nor Coronation to conduct, but his hereditary office brought him much other work of lower profile. His military background and interest in history, as well as his heredity, made him ideally suited for this particular job. His rehearsals of state ceremonial were a treat much treasured by those who took part, the military commands ameliorated by his brand of humour: 'Now look here, Lord Chancellor ... Don't worry, the worse the rehearsal, the better it will be on the day' – and so it always was. The business in hand was leavened by short historical interpolations and explanations: 'Now Black Rod will go to fetch the Commons, but they won't let him into the Chamber because of Charles I ... quite right too! Now Black Rod, off you go.'

The Earl Marshal is one of the great officers of state, like the Lord High Constable, the Lord High Steward and the Lord Great Chamberlain. Many of these medieval dignities have fallen into partial abeyance, like that of the Lord High Constable, a post which is only resurrected for Coronation day. Others have become largely ceremonial, as in the case of the Lord Great Chamberlain where the day-to-day work is executed by a deputy at Court, the Lord Chamberlain, but the Earl Marshal still has an active role under the Crown with responsibility for state ceremonial, especially the annual State Opening of Parliament as

well as rehearsals, supervision of the College of Arms and overseeing
all new grants of arms. No new arms can be granted by the Kings of
Arms in England and Wales, and parts of the Commonwealth, without
the Earl Marshal's signed warrant. The Earl Marshal is also responsible
for approving the annual budget of the College, and for new appoint-
ments of officers of arms, making individual recommendations to the
Sovereign for officers in ordinary (by Royal Warrant) and officers
extraordinary (by Royal Sign Manual). The Earl Marshal is the last of
the medieval English Officers of State to play such an executive role.

The office of Marshal evolved originally as deputy to the Constable
and was responsible for the Court as a battle horde acting as judge in
the military court of arms (later Earl Marshal's Court) and responsible
for outdoor processions and parades. The position emerged as early as
the reign of Henry I when John son of Gilbert claimed the office and
took Marshal as his surname. On the extinction of the Marshal line the
king gave the Marshal's baton to the eldest co-heir: the Bigod Earls of
Norfolk. From that time on, despite attainders and other interruptions,
the Marshalship has mainly been associated with the Norfolk title.
After the surrender of the office by the last Bigod Earl of Norfolk, it was
given by Edward II to his younger brother Thomas of Brotherton, Earl
of Norfolk (Miles's ancestor) in 1316. Richard II granted the Marshalship to Thomas Mowbray 1st Duke of Norfolk who was also titled Earl
Marshal. In 1483, when John Lord Howard (senior co-heir to the
Mowbrays) was created 1st Duke of Norfolk (of the Howard line) by
Richard III, he was also created Earl Marshal and subsequent Dukes of
Norfolk have been Earl Marshal, though the dignity did not become
hereditary in the Howard family until 1672, when Charles II made the
future 6th Duke hereditary Earl Marshal of England.

The Dukes, as Catholics, in the eighteenth century were unable to
exercise their powers but were allowed to appoint Deputies from
among the Protestant branches of the Howard family tree to act for
them, and thus the Earl of Carlisle and Earl of Suffolk acted in this role.
The 12th Duke appointed his younger brother Lord Henry Howard
Molyneux Howard (who had been brought up in his mother's Anglican religion) as his Deputy Earl Marshal. On Lord Henry's death in
1824, the 12th Duke brought in his own private bill to enable him to
exercise his role as Earl Marshal though a papist. This was to 'test the
bath water' for the Catholic Emancipation Act, and when The Duke's

Act passed through Parliament unhindered, it became evident that
Emancipation could follow, as it did in 1829.

Miles was fascinated by the history of his hereditary office and was
proud of it, not in a personal or possessive way, but rather like somebody who lives in an ancient listed building, taking an intelligent interest in it and telling visitors about it. At the annual State Opening of
Parliament he wore the peer's parliamentary robe made for the 12th
Duke on taking his seat in the Lords immediately after the Emancipation Act in 1829, the first Catholic peer to sit there since the Act of
Exclusion in 1677, and which every Duke of Norfolk has worn since.
He liked to tell the joke of The Duke of Edinburgh saying 'Miles, those
robes are getting very old and scruffy. They need a good press.' The
gold Earl Marshal's baton he carried had been presented to the same
12th Duke by Queen Victoria at her Coronation in 1838.

He tackled the College of Arms with his usual energy, helping with
fund-raising in the United States as well as England, and instigating the
repair of the building in time for the quincentenary of the College in
1984. Miles in the course of his time as Earl Marshal worked with four
successive Garter Kings of Arms: Sir Anthony Wagner, Lieutenant
Colonel Sir Colin Cole, Sir Conrad Swan and Peter Gwynn-Jones, the
present incumbent. All had different strengths. Wagner was an Etonian
scholar and a good moneyman but somewhat shy and introverted.
Colin cut a swashbuckling military dash and was outgoing but held an
easy rein on matters of detail. Swan was also a scholar but perhaps had
an over-romantic view of heraldry and genealogy and retired early,
while Gwynn-Jones was efficient. Miles treated them and the other
senior heralds as his staff officers. He formulated strategies, encouraged,
advised and supported but left them to get on with the implementation.

This had notable successes, especially with the reserved but compe-
tent Anthony Wagner. The latter put the College's finances on a sound
structural footing and set up the College of Arms Trust, a charitable
fund to maintain the building and the College Records, the most
complete and important body of heraldic material in existence. The
College building, on the site of medieval Derby House, had been given
to the Heralds by Queen Mary Tudor and rebuilt after the Great Fire in
the late seventeenth century. By the 1970s it was showing its age, but
the College had never had any endowment. Under Miles's chairmanship, the College of Arms Trust not only raised the money for renewing

the roof and repairing all the external brickwork, but built up a substantial reserve fund. The buildings, thanks to Miles's efforts, are in a better condition today than for a century or more.

Another great success was the Heralds' Museum established in the Royal Armouries at the Tower of London. This was the brainchild of Anthony Wagner, John Brooke-Little and Rodney Dennys. The original idea had been to build a purpose-designed museum on the north side of the College, abutting St Paul's Steps, but this proved to be too expensive. The Tower alternative was an ideal solution, for it benefited from the large numbers of tourists there. Apart from displaying changing exhibitions of heraldic material from the Heralds' Records, the Museum was also an excellent money earner for the College of Arms Trust. The arrangement worked very well for a number of years but finally came to an end when the Armouries moved to Leeds and no suitable alternative venue could be found for the Heralds' exhibition.

In his duties as Earl Marshal, Miles was ably assisted by two successive Earl Marshal's Secretaries, Sir Walter Verco and Patrick Dickinson. Verco had joined the College as a boy and worked his way up the hierarchy by dint of native intelligence and hard work. He knew his subject backwards and was highly efficient, a quality which Miles always prized. Patrick Dickinson was an Oxford graduate (and former President of the Union) who was also efficient. They organised the annual State Opening of Parliament impeccably, and prepared the patents for grants of arms and other routine business, calling on Miles in Clabon Mews when he did not come to the College, though he visited regularly.

Miles's time as Earl Marshal overlapped with the long years of Conservative government from 1978 to 1997 and there were no threats to downgrade or alter the historic state opening procession (dating from the late fifteenth and early sixteenth centuries). With the advent of the Labour government in 1997 there was a feeling in some corners that the ceremonial should be shorn and 'modernised'. Miles was extremely adept in deflecting these proposals for change and was insistent that the heralds and other historic elements should continue. It is thanks to him that the annual State Opening of Parliament remains the ceremonial highpoint of the English Constitution.

Apart from his hereditary role as Earl Marshal, and his active involvement in the House of Lords (which has been described elsewhere), Miles took on other public duties. Some were largely 'presidential' like the patronage of nearly 200 local organisations and societies in the 'Howard lands' of Yorkshire, Norfolk and Sussex, some of which he took on from his predecessor, others reflecting his own personal interests and enthusiasms. His historical enthusiasms, for instance, were reflected in his chairmanship of the Marc Fitch Fund, a charity established to give grants for local history research and publication and genealogical studies, and in which he became involved through Francis Steer and Anthony Wagner who were old friends of the founder, Marc Fitch. Another natural progression was his role in the Fishmongers. He had been put up for the Fishmongers' Company by his father-in-law Gerald Constable Maxwell many years earlier. He became Prime Warden in the quincentennial year of the dukedom in 1983.

Another, perhaps at first sight surprising, role he took on was the presidency of the British Building Societies. This, however, was a reflection of his firm commitment to the family as a social institution. He was a strong believer in the traditional Christian idea of the family, and considered it important therefore that young couples should be able to buy their own homes easily. Building Societies with their straightforward system of mortgage provision seemed the best way to achieve this, and he gave them his full support.

His particular position as Earl Marshal and lay-leader of the English Catholics led to his representing the Queen when meeting or dealing with the Pope on several historic occasions. He was the royal representative at the funerals in Rome of Popes Paul VI and John Paul I and the enthronement of Pope John Paul I and the present Pope John Paul II. When Pope John Paul II came to Britain in 1982, Miles met him, as the Sovereign's representative, at Gatwick Airport. This role as special ambassador from the British Crown to the Papacy continued a tradition which had emerged in the late nineteenth century under Queen Victoria and the 15th Duke, and which particularly suited Miles with his active Catholic commitments and personal loyalty to the monarch. He was recognised for his achievements by The Queen, who made him a Knight of the Garter, GCVO, and gave him the Royal Victorian Chain on his retirement in 2000.

Index